THE VOLATILITY COURSE WORKBOOK

Founded in 1807, John Wiley & Sons is the oldest independent publishing company in the United States. With offices in North America, Europe, Australia and Asia, Wiley is globally committed to developing and marketing print and electronic products and services for our customers' professional and personal knowledge and understanding.

The Wiley Trading series features books by traders who have survived the market's ever changing temperament and have prospered—some by reinventing systems, others by getting back to basics. Whether a novice trader, professional, or somewhere in-between, these books will provide the advice and strategies needed to prosper today and well into the future.

For a list of available titles, please visit our web site at www.WileyFinance.com.

THE VOLATILITY COURSE WORKBOOK

Step-by-Step Exercises to Help You Master *The Volatility Course*

George A. Fontanills
Tom Gentile

JOHN WILEY & SONS, INC.

Published by John Wiley & Sons, Inc., Hoboken, New Jersey.
Published simultaneously in Canada.

For general information on our other products and services, or technical support, please contact our Customer Care Department within the United States at 800-762-2974, outside the United States at 317-572-3993 or fax 317-572-4002.

Wiley also publishes its books in a variety of electronic formats. Some content that appears in print may not be available in electronic books.

For more information about Wiley products, visit our web site at www.wiley.com.

ISBN 0-471-39817-9

Printed in the United States of America.

10 9 8 7 6 5 4 3

It is with great love
that we dedicate this book to
Alexandria, Benjamin, and Christina Cawood.

Disclaimer
Hypothetical or simulated performance results have certain limitations. Unlike an actual performance record, simulated results do not represent actual trading. Also, since the trades have not actually been executed, the results may have under- or overcompensated for the impact, if any, of certain factors, such as lack of liquidity. Simulated trading programs in general are also subject to the fact that they are designed with the benefit of hindsight. No representation is being made that any account will or is likely to achieve profits or losses similar to those shown. There is a risk of loss in all forms of trading.

Important Notice
Trading stocks and options has large potential rewards, but also large potential risks. You must be aware of the risks and willing to accept them in order to invest in the markets. Do not trade with money you cannot afford to lose. This is neither a solicitation nor an offer to buy or sell stocks or options. This book is published for educational purposes only and should not be relied upon for current prices, for example. Consult a licensed professional about your individual trading. Prior to buying or selling an option, you should receive from your brokerage firm a copy of *Characteristics and Risks of Standardized Options*. Copies of this document are also available from the Chicago Board Options Exchange, 400 South La Salle Street, Chicago, IL 60605; or it can be viewed at the CBOE web site at www.cboe.com or at www.optionetics.com.

Contents

Questions and Exercises

1

Crisis and Chaos in Financial Markets

Summary

Most investors understand that, historically, stock prices rise. This has been the case ever since securities started trading after the signing of the Buttonwood Agreement in 1792. It is undeniable that, over time, stocks appreciate. At the same time, however, there are times when stocks do not perform well. So-called bear markets surface periodically in which stock prices fall and shareholders lose money. In addition, sometimes the stock market's decline can be violent, such as the crash of 1987—an extreme example. That sharp market decline stands out in the history books as a period of extreme volatility and lost wealth for stock market investors.

The volatility trader has a different perspective on the market than the traditional stock market investor. The volatility trader understands that times of falling stock prices and rising volatility are inevitable. However, periods of high volatility offer an equal number of trading opportunities as when stock prices are rising. Therefore, volatility is not a negative. There are ways to profit regardless of market direction, and volatility is not a nemesis. Instead, volatility can offer some of the best financial rewards to the savvy trader.

Recent events highlight the value in trading volatility rather than blindly buying stocks and hoping they increase in value. In the fall of 1998, financial markets around the globe were rattled in a widespread panic. A short time later, after a surge in technology stocks and the creation of a speculative bubble in Internet stocks, the floor caved in and stocks suffered sharp declines for more than 18 months. By the middle of the year 2001, many companies saw their share prices trade at fractions of their year 2000 peaks. Then, in September 2001, the U.S. stock market suffered another blow when terrorists attacked the heart of the world's financial center—

downtown Manhattan. All of these events, in less than five years, served to highlight some of the risks investors face. Some were economic, some political, and others military. Nevertheless, they all made the traditional approach to investing a gut-wrenching experience.

While trading volatility makes a great deal of sense given the complex nature of the stock market today and the myriad of uncertainties investors face, it is not a passive approach to the market. The volatility trader is actively involved in the day-to-day activity of the market. This does not necessarily mean trading every day and losing sleep at night due to the uncertainty of financial markets. However, it does require a certain time commitment that is not needed when simply buying stocks in anticipation that the market will be higher 10 years from now than it is today.

The savvy volatility trader understands the following key principles:

- Falling stock prices occur roughly one-third of the time.
- Profits can be made regardless of whether stocks are rising or falling.
- Volatility is a fact of life when investing.
- There are times when volatility in the stock market is high and makes the headlines in the financial press.
- There are times when volatility is low.
- Whether volatility is high or low, however, there are ways to generate profits using the strategies outlined in *The Volatility Course*.

Questions and Exercises

1. The U.S. stock market suffered its greatest point decline in history on ____________.

   A. October 29, 1929
   B. October 19, 1987
   C. April 4, 2000
   D. September 17, 2001

2. True or False: The bear market that preceded the Great Depression of the 1930s began on September 29, 1929, and lasted until June 1938.

3. What is an index, and why are indexes helpful when it comes to studying the stock market?

   ____

   ____

4. True or False: Rising interest rates hurt stock market investors.

5. The primary goal of the Federal Reserve is to ___________.
   A. Stabilize prices
   B. Promote economic growth
   C. Strive for full employment
   D. All of the above

6. Prior to the market slide from September 2000 until September 2001, the market was vulnerable and eventually collapsed because of ___________.
   A. Overpriced Internet stocks
   B. Excess speculative activity on the part of individual investors
   C. Rising interest rates
   D. Global economic decline
   E. All of the above

7. As a general rule, a bull market is identified by a ___________ rise from a low in the Dow Jones Industrial Average or other measure of the market.
   A. 10%
   B. 15%
   C. 20%
   D. 25%

8. As a general rule, a bear market is identified by a ___________ decline from a high in the Dow Jones Industrial Average or other measure of the market.
   A. 10%
   B. 15%
   C. 20%
   D. 25%

9. Can volatility in one financial market spread to other markets, or does it remain isolated? Why?

   ____

   ____

10. True or False: Ultimately, the stock market falls more than it rises.

11. The world's largest auction-style stock exchange dates back to the Buttonwood Agreement of 1792. Today it is known as the ___________.
    A. New York Stock Exchange
    B. American Stock Exchange
    C. Philadelphia Stock Exchange

12. True or False: Volatility equals risk.

13. True or False: It is usually profitable to bet against the financial system over the long term.

14. Briefly describe why rising and falling markets are named "bull" and "bear."

 ____

 ____

Media Assignment

There are a number of different media tools available to the option strategist today—financial newspapers, magazines, the Internet, and television. The most valuable, by far, is the Internet. Today, while the cost of a personal computer has fallen dramatically, its speed, memory, and efficiency have enjoyed explosive growth. In addition, the proliferation of financial-related Internet sites coupled with the new high-speed Internet access capabilities (cable, DSL, broadband, etc.) have made tasks that once took hours possible in only minutes. There is no question that Internet access and subscriptions to a few key services greatly facilitate the process of identifying and implementing efficient option strategies.

While the Internet is the most important tool available to the option strategist today, this chapter focuses on events that cause volatility in the stock market, and following these events does not necessarily require the use of a computer. The chapter is concerned largely with the financial press in *all* its forms—television, radio, print, Web-based, and so on. Therefore, the first media assignment requires access to financial-related news services. These include, but are not limited to, financial television programs such as the *Nightly Business Report* on PBS, and *Moneyline* on CNN, and newspapers like the *Wall Street Journal*, the *Financial Times*, and *Investor's Business Daily*, along with Web-based financial news from Bloomberg.com, Yahoo! Finance, and Optionetics.com.

When evaluating the financial press, the reader is trying to answer the question, "What is moving the markets?" As described in Chapter 1 of *The Volatility Course*, there are a number of different factors that can trigger periods of volatility. Some stem from the stock market itself—such as earnings, concerns over corporate accounting, or stock mergers. Others are economic in nature and include changes in interest rates, energy prices, or economic growth. Finally, some events fall outside of finance altogether, but still rattle the nerves of investors. The terrorist attacks of September 11, 2001, are the most recent example, but there are others. Wars, politics, and other noneconomic events can all shake investor nerves.

The goal of the first media assignment, then, is to uncover what factors are driving the markets higher or lower on a day-to-day basis. To accomplish this assignment, start a trading journal. Each day, try to write a short account of the day's significant events and their apparent effects on the financial and business community. Keep in mind when doing so, however, that investors do not always react correctly. In addition, when markets begin to swing wildly the media often adds to the situation by dramatizing it since the financial press receives a lot more interest from market watchers when the situation appears chaotic and out of control. During those times, the option strategist must be careful not to get caught up in the excitement of short-term events, and to focus on the bigger picture instead. While it is important to understand what is moving the markets, the strategist must be able to stay emotionally detached from the situation in order to keep thought processes clear. If not, investment decisions are likely to be made out of fear or greed, rather than based on rational decision making.

Vocabulary List

Please define the following terms:

- Bear market
- Black Tuesday
- Bloody Monday
- Bull market
- Buy and hold
- Chicago Board Options Exchange (CBOE)
- Commodities
- Contagion
- Correction
- Dow Jones Industrial Average
- Exchange-traded fund (ETF)
- Federal Reserve
- Fed funds rate
- Futures markets
- Global financial crisis
- Index fund
- Liquidity
- Long Term Capital Management
- Margin
- Margin call
- Mutual fund
- Nifty Fifty
- Options
- Prime rate
- Pullback
- S&P 500

2

Volatility in the Stock Market

Summary

The stock market is a fascinating place. Its day-to-day movements reflect the buying and selling decisions of millions of investors around the world. Often trading is orderly and uneventful. During periods of quiet trading, investors develop a sense of safety and comfort. There is nothing to worry about, and the action of the market gets no coverage from the mainstream press. At other times, however, investors are rattled. News events, crises, and panic cause stock prices to fall, sometimes quite rapidly. During those times, the term "volatility" begins to surface on the evening news. Yet, while volatility is often associated with falling stock prices, a rising market can also sometimes be characterized as having high volatility—for example, when stocks are skyrocketing and investors are reacting out of optimism and greed. Basically, periods of high volatility are often the result of an emotionally driven market. The two key emotions are fear and greed; they can cause stocks to have high volatility when moving higher or lower. The successful volatility trader remains emotionless and understands that market volatility does not mean lost wealth. No matter what the market delivers, the volatility trader is prepared and ready to take advantage of the unique trading opportunities various states of market volatility foster.

While increasing volatility generally is a result of changes in investor emotions and psychology in the marketplace, it does not occur in a vacuum. That is, investors are continually absorbing new information concerning the outlook for individual companies, industries, and the economy. As information arrives, investment decisions are made. When there are no unusual occurrences, stocks can trade quietly for long periods of time. Volatility will remain low. But if investors are taken aback by events, there is often an impulsive or knee-jerk reaction. In addition, there is a tendency for investors to trade with the trend. They are attracted to moving prices. Therefore, when news events drive investors to react emotionally, stocks begin heading in one direction or another, and this often leads to herdlike behavior or the bandwagon effect. It takes a combination of new information and emotion to trigger high levels of market volatility.

Obviously, understanding that volatility can change from one moment to the next is not enough information to trade for profits. Among other things, the options trader needs a means of quantifying volatility. Tools for doing so are discussed in later chapters. Before that, it is important to understand how stock and index prices are determined and disseminated, because all measures of volatility are derived from prices—generally the closing values. Therefore, this chapter covers some of the basics of trading like stocks, indexes, quotes, and basic definitions of volatility.

Questions and Exercises

1. Name the three indexes (and their ticker symbols) reporters most often use to comment on the performance of the stock market.
   1. ____________________
   2. ____________________
   3. ____________________
2. By recent estimates ____________ of all American households own stocks in one form or another today.
   A. 30%
   B. 40%
   C. 50%
   D. 60%
3. When a company wants to start selling shares of stock to the public, it issues the ____________.
   A. Initial public offering (IPO)
   B. Venture capital shares
   C. Publicly traded preferred stock shares
4. Name the three principal stock exchanges.
   1. ____________________
   2. ____________________
   3. ____________________
5. As an off-floor trader, you buy at the ____________ price and sell at the ____________ price.
   A. Ask/Bid
   B. Offer/Ask
   C. Bid/Ask

6. Match the terms with their respective definitions in Table 2.1.

Table 2.1 Match Term to Definition

Data	*Definition*
Last	A. The highest price a prospective buyer (floor trader) is prepared to pay for a specified time for a trading unit of a specified security.
Open	B. The highest price for the current trading day.
Change	C. The percentage the price has changed since the previous day's closing price.
% Change	D. The bottom line (net pretax profit) divided by the number of shares outstanding.
High	E. The last price that the security traded for at the exchange.
Low	F. The lowest price acceptable to a prospective seller (floor trader) of a security.
Bid	G. The total number of shares the company has issued.
Ask	H. The price of the first transaction of the current trading day.
52-Week High	I. The total number of shares traded in a day.
52-Week Low	J. This indicates where a company lists, or registers, its shares.
Earnings per Share	K. The lowest price the stock traded at in the past 52-week period.
Volume	L. Stock price divided by the earnings per share.
Shares Outstanding	M. The lowest price for the current trading day.
Market Cap	N. The amount the last sale differs from the previous trading day's closing price.
P/E Ratio	O. The highest price the stock traded at in the past 52-week period.
Exchange	P. Shares outstanding multiplied by the closing stock price.

7. The purpose of computing an index is to measure the performance of ____________.

   A. An entire group of stocks

   B. A specific sector of stocks

   C. A specific industrial sector of stocks

   D. All of the above

8. True or False: The Russell 2000 is an index that primarily tracks the performance of small cap stocks.

9. True or False: An index can be used as an investment.

10. Match the indexes with their respective ticker symbols in Table 2.2.

Table 2.2 Match Index to Symbol

Index Name	*Symbol*
Dow Jones Industrial Average	$NYA
S&P 500	$COMPQ
Wilshire 5000	$TMW
New York Stock Exchange Composite	$OEX
Nasdaq Composite	$RUA
S&P 100	$INDU
Russell 3000	$SPX

11. ETF stands for ____________.
    A. Electronic trading funds
    B. Exchange trust funds
    C. Equity trading funds
    D. Exchange-traded funds

12. Investors seeking to own a basket of stocks that consists of mostly technology stocks can buy shares of ____________.
    A. DIA
    B. SPY
    C. QQQ
    D. IWM

13. What is the difference between HOLDRs and ETFs?

    ____

    ____

14. The most important factor in determining an asset's volatility is ____________.
    A. Volume of shares traded
    B. Price changes
    C. Price changes in one business day
    D. Option premiums

15. The ____________ is the most common price used for computing volatility.
    A. Opening price
    B. Closing price

16. When there are long bars between high and low prices on a stock chart, volatility is ____________.
    A. High
    B. Low
    C. Neutral

17. When important and relevant new information arrives to the market, volatility tends to ____________.
    A. Rise
    B. Fall
    C. Remain neutral
18. True or False: Human emotion has no effect on volatility.
19. Name and describe two ways of measuring volatility.
    1. ____
    2. ____
20. The most common reason for a stock to fall precipitously is due to concern over ____________.
    A. Mergers
    B. Earnings
    C. Accounting irregularities
    D. Employee cuts

Media Assignment

The media assignment from Chapter 1 focused on the financial press and developing an understanding of the factors that cause changes in stock market volatility. Of course, there are different types of events that can cause stock prices to change rapidly. All develop when new information hits the market. For instance, an earnings report—positive or negative—from an important company such as General Electric, Intel, or Microsoft, can have a marketwide impact. Other economic events, political uncertainty, or military conflicts can also cause investors to change their expectations and can lead to frantic buying or selling in the stock market. As these events unfold, it is paramount to have a long-term operating framework, understand and digest the news without reacting emotionally, and make investment decisions accordingly.

Now, before actually establishing trades, the strategist must have an understanding of the basics of the stock market. For example, if volatility is increasing, how do we know? Obviously, during periods of high volatility, stock prices and the market will move dramatically higher or lower. But how do we quantify these changes? The answer: stock quotes. All traders have access to quotes. There are two kinds. First, a number of web sites and financial publications offer free quotes. If the trader uses print publications, such as the *Wall Street Journal* or *Investor's Business Daily*, the quotes will reflect the previous day's closing prices. Looking through the stock tables alphabetically, the trader can find price information from the previous day's market session.

While sifting through lengthy quote tables in print publications was the most common method for finding quotes a decade ago, it no longer is. Today, Internet access makes it possible to obtain stock quotes throughout the day from a multitude of web sites. There is no shortage of finance-based sites with free quotes, including Yahoo! Finance, Bloomberg.com, Optionetics.com, and a variety of others. Generally, free quotes on the Internet are available throughout the day, but are delayed 15 to 20 minutes. Live, or real-time quotes, which show trades as they happen, are also available on a number of different Internet sites, but for a fee. Additionally, some online brokerage firms allow clients access to real-time quotes.

This media assignment encourages readers to find a quote service that fits his or her budget and trading experience. If you trade five or more times a week, it makes sense to invest in some type of real-time quote service. Being able to see live data and prices can often lead to better trades. More importantly, however, any options trader should have the capability to find quotes for any stock or option with relative ease. Outside of the printed publications, some sites worth exploring include the Chicago Board Options Exchange (www.cboe.com), the Nasdaq (www.nasdaq.com), Optionetics.com (www.optionetics.com), and Yahoo! Finance (http://finance.yahoo.com). All of these sites provide delayed market quotes and news at no charge.

Once you find a site that fits your needs, take the time to follow a stock and a few of its options. Become familiar with stock tickers and option symbols and watch how their prices change over time. How do the changes in price relate to scheduled and unscheduled news events? How does the option price change in relation to changes in the underlying asset? Keep a log of these changes in your trading journal.

Vocabulary List

Please define the following terms:

- Ask
- Bid
- Closing price
- Comovement
- Derivative instruments
- Historical volatility
- HOLDRs
- Implied volatility (IV)
- Index
- Initial public offering (IPO)
- Listing requirements
- Moving average
- Open
- Private company
- Public company
- Securities and Exchange Commission (SEC)
- Spread
- Stock
- Stock symbol

3

Historical Volatility

Summary

The volatility of any stock or market changes over time. It is rarely stagnant and is often in a state of flux. Spotting periods of high volatility is relatively easy for the trader to do. A stock chart showing sharp moves higher or lower suggests that the stock or market has been exhibiting high levels of volatility. Periods of low volatility and quiet trading are also relatively easy to identify. When a stock is trading sideways, moderately lower, gradually higher, or within a narrow range, volatility is considered low. For the volatility trader, understanding that volatility is always changing and identifying extreme highs and lows is not enough. The trader must also be able to quantify volatility using an objective measure.

Historical volatility offers a means of gauging a stock or a market's volatility. As the name suggests, it measures the levels of volatility that have existed in the past. There are a number of ways of computing historical volatility, but the most common method is to use a measure known as statistical volatility—which is the annualized standard deviation of a stock's closing prices over a period of days (10, 20, 90, etc.). Statistical volatility is expressed as a percentage. For example, a stock with a 20-day statistical volatility of 100% has been relatively volatile, while statistical volatility of 20% suggests relatively quiet trading.

Chapter 3 also introduces three other measures of historical volatility that can help make sense of a stock's past price movements. In addition to statistical volatility, the chapter introduces the reader to Average True Range (ATR), beta, and Bollinger bands. Each provides a unique view of historical volatility.

Using indicators such as Average True Range and Bollinger bands, as well as finding the statistical volatility of a stock or index, is easy to do in today's markets. The days of searching through financial papers for relevant information are a thing of the past. The trader today has enormous resources at his or her disposal simply with a personal computer and an Internet connection. This includes relatively simple (but important) tasks, such as pulling up stock quotes or creating stock charts, and more complex analyses like viewing statistical volatility over time or adding Bollinger bands to a graph. Indeed, technology and the personal computer are paramount to successfully trading volatility.

Questions and Exercises

1. True or False: When prices are rising and the majority of investors are making money, emotion (optimism and greed) drives prices lower.
2. True or False: When prices are falling, emotion (fear and panic) drives prices higher.
3. Historical volatility is also referred to as ___________.
   A. Statistical volatility
   B. Actual volatility
   C. Implied volatility
   D. Past volatility
   E. A and B
   F. A and D
4. True or False: Historical volatility is computed using current stock prices.
5. Historical volatility measures a stock's propensity for ___________.
   A. Change in volume
   B. Rising to new highs
   C. A breakout
   D. Price movement
6. Implied volatility is priced into an option's value in the ___________.
   A. Past
   B. Present
   C. Future
7. When studying statistical volatility, it is important to consider it in light of ___________.
   A. Other stocks or indexes
   B. Past levels of historical volatility associated with that stock or index
   C. Historical volatility within different time frames
   D. All of the above
8. True or False: Average True Range is exactly the same as statistical volatility.

9. Moving averages are used to analyze ____________ over a specified period of time on an average basis.
   A. Volume
   B. Price action
   C. Earnings
   D. Indexes

10. Bollinger bands are moving ____________.
    A. Averages
    B. Closing prices
    C. Standard deviations
    D. Candlesticks

11. When analyzing Bollinger bands, the trading strategist expects the bands will come together when the movement in the stock is ____________ volatile.
    A. More
    B. Less
    C. Consistently

12. When the movement of a stock becomes more volatile, Bollinger bands will become ____________.
    A. Narrower
    B. Wider

13. True or False: A high beta stock is a high volatility stock and subject to greater percentage moves than the overall market.

Media Assignment

The media assignment from Chapter 2 centered around finding price information for stocks, indexes, and options. In order to do so, the first step is to find the appropriate symbols. Once the symbol is known, a number of different web sites offer free price quotes. More active traders will want to subscribe to a real-time quote service. Doing so will provide more timely information and also avoid the hassle of retrieving one quote at a time. Real-time quote services provide the capability of creating windows with multiple quotes that are updated as trades happen. The question of which quote service to subscribe to is an individual decision that depends on a number of factors including how much an individual trades, the willingness to spend money on a subscription fee, and the technological capabilities available to the trader.

Now, however, the reader wants to move on to another one of the basics of trading—stock charts. Therefore, the purpose of this media assignment is to become adept at using stock charts and applying indicators. There are a number of ways to create stock charts. Several years ago, analysts were limited to buying charts from financial publication companies or creating them by hand. Today, the process is much easier. A number of web sites offer stock charting capabilities—including the Interactive Wall Street Journal (interactive.WSJ.com), Bloomberg.com, Stockcharts.com, BigCharts.com, Optionetics.com, and others. Many brokerage firms have charting capabilities available to account holders. In addition, it is possible to buy charting software from companies such as Omega Research and Trading Techniques.

Whether using free trading capabilities online or using a more sophisticated software package, the goal behind the latest media assignment is to begin using charts on a regular basis. Choose a handful of stocks that are actively traded. Chart them and change the time frames on the charts—from daily to weekly to monthly. Understand that a trend can go from an uptrend to a downtrend depending on the time frame used in a chart. For example, what appears to be an uptrend on a daily chart could well be a downtrend on the monthly chart. As a rule, the chartist defers to the trend encompassing the longer time frame. Also, note the stock's volatility. If trading is orderly in a well-defined range, the chart will reflect that and suggest the stock is exhibiting low volatility. In contrast, a chart with many peaks and valleys suggests high volatility. Basically, charts can provide information regarding a stock's trend and volatility in a quick and effective manner.

Next, apply indicators to the chart. Some of the indicators discussed in this chapter are volume, moving averages, Bollinger bands, and Average True Range. These are common indicators that can be applied to charts using almost any software program or Web-based charting tools. Use the indicators described in the chapter with a number of different stocks and consider how each helps identify turning points in different situations. In sum, begin charting stocks and applying indicators. Doing so will give you a quick and easy way to see the price action and volatility of the stock and help you to make more timely trades. Once again, keep a log of your charting experimentation so that you can record the lessons learned.

Vocabulary List

Please define the following terms:

- Average True Range (ATR)
- Beta
- Bollinger bands
- Standard deviation
- Statistical volatility

4

Trading Historical Volatility

Summary

This chapter introduces a number of ways to measure historical volatility: statistical volatility, ATR, Bollinger bands, and beta. Each offers information regarding a stock or market's past level of volatility. Each measure, in turn, is unique. For instance, statistical volatility uses the standard deviation of past stock prices over a period of time. When a stock or index swings wildly, statistical volatility will rise; during periods of quiet and low volatility, statistical volatility falls. Statistical volatility (and other measures of historical volatility) gauge whether a stock has been trading quietly and in a narrow range, or with wide swings and extreme price changes. In this chapter, the reader wants to consider how each measure of historical volatility can be used to develop trading strategies.

Volatility is always in a state of flux. Traders, therefore, want to consider historical volatility over different time frames. The goal is to identify an average or normal range for each individual stock or index. Unusual periods of high or low volatility become more obvious when considering an average value of historical volatility over a period of time. For example, if it is known that the average volatility of IBM stock over the past 100 days is 35%, but over the past 10 days it has risen to 100%, the large increase suggests that volatility is moving out of its normal range. At that point, the questions facing the volatility trader are: Has the historical volatility of IBM deviated too far outside of its normal range? Will it fall back?

To answer those questions, the volatility trader has to keep in mind an important factor: reversion to the mean. Even though historical volatility is always changing, most stocks or indexes have a normal or average value. When volatility diverges greatly from that normal range, there is a tendency for it to revert back to that average, or mean. Looking at historical volatility over time allows the trader to assign a normal range. Extreme deviations are generally followed by a reversion toward the average and, therefore, profit opportunities for the volatility trader who anticipates the price move. The measures of historical volatility discussed in the previous chapter—ATR, Bollinger bands, and statistical volatility—can be used to determine what a stock or index's normal level of volatility is and to pinpoint trading opportunities by exploiting the phenomenon known as reversion to the mean. In the last three chapters of *The Volatility Course*, specific option strategies are outlined to help in this endeavor.

Questions and Exercises

1. When prices are falling, fear and panic can overwhelm investors, which drives prices ____________.
   A. Higher
   B. Lower
   C. To trade within a range
2. When prices are rising and the majority of investors are making money, optimism and greed drive prices ____________.
   A. Higher
   B. Lower
   C. To trade within a range
3. True or False: Historical volatility is computed using past stock prices and the Black-Scholes option pricing model.
4. The most common method of measuring historical volatility is ____________.
   A. Computed volatility
   B. Implied volatility
   C. Realized volatility
   D. Statistical volatility
5. True or False: If a stock or an index fluctuates wildly in price, it is said to have high historical volatility, which could lead to lower option premiums.
6. To make a determination as to what is normal for a particular stock or index, traders must consider historical volatility using ____________.
   A. Bollinger bands
   B. Average True Range
   C. Different time frames
   D. Standard deviations

7. Although historical volatility is always in a state of change, most stocks or indexes can be assigned a normal or average value. When volatility diverges greatly from that normal range, there is a tendency for it to revert back to that average. This is referred to as ___________.

   A. A correction

   B. Reversion to the mean

   C. The equilibrium level

   D. All of the above

8. There are only two factors under consideration when computing moving averages: the stock price and ___________.

   A. Volume of shares traded

   B. Number of days

   C. Support levels

   D. Resistance levels

9. True or False: Fifty- or 200-day moving averages are commonly used for studying short-term trends with regard to a stock or an index.

10. In general, a "buy" signal is triggered when the moving average begins an upward slope and the stock price closes ___________ it.

    A. Above

    B. Below

11. True or False: Generally, the shorter the time period used in the moving average, the greater the number of "buy" and "sell" signals.

12. ___________ is the price level at which a stock price attracts a significant amount of demand—the type of buying that can stop a downward slide in a stock price.

    A. Support

    B. Resistance

    C. Equilibrium

13. ___________ is a price level at which a stock or index has witnessed great amounts of supply and can no longer move higher.

    A. Support

    B. Resistance

    C. Equilibrium

14. True or False: At first, it is best to use 9 days or 18 days for moving averages because nearly every software program out there has these set as defaults in their systems.

15. During periods of high volatility, if the 50-day moving average pulls back to the 200-day moving average, this sets up a nice ____________ signal for the stock.

    A. Buy

    B. Sell

16. True or False: When movement in the stock price is steady and less volatile, Bollinger bands tend to diverge or widen; when the movement of the stock or index begins to swing wildly and volatility rises, the bands tend to come together and become narrow.

17. If a stock price moves above two standard deviations from its normal range, the stock is then considered ____________, and its price is due to fall back toward its moving average and correct.

    A. Oversold

    B. Overbought

18. Using Bollinger bands, how can you tell if the stock or index is ripe for a breakout?

    ____

    ____

19. True or False: Historical volatility can be used to gauge when a stock is likely to get quiet or explosive by comparing 10-day to 90-day time frames. A very low 10/90 ratio suggests that the underlying stock is consolidating.

20. The advantage of the ATR over statistical volatility is that it accounts for not only the closing price of a stock or option, but also ____________.

    A. The current volume levels

    B. The overbought and oversold conditions

    C. The current highs and lows

    D. All of the above

21. If a stock opens significantly ____________ than the previous day's closing level, it is known as a "gap up."

    A. Higher

    B. Lower

22. True or False: When ATR rises to extreme highs, the path of least resistance is to the upside, and chances are the stock will rise even higher.

Media Assignment

Looking at historical volatility over time allows the trader to assign a normal range to a stock or an index. Extreme deviations from this normal range are generally followed by a reversion toward the average. ATR, Bollinger bands, and statistical volatility have all been discussed as tools for measuring a stock's or an index's volatility. Each can be used to determine what a security's normal level of volatility is. When a stock deviates significantly from that average range, look for opportunistic trading situations. Again, the goal is to take advantage of reversion to the mean, which is the most important concept discussed in this chapter on trading historical volatility.

So far, the media assignments have focused on the financial press, obtaining quotes, creating stock charts, and applying indicators. Now, the reader wants to begin paper trading. For those who have never heard that term, paper trading is really pretend investing. It is analogous to a pilot training inside a simulator instead of actually flying an airplane. How is this done? Simple. Rather than calling a broker or actually entering an online trade, the trader simply writes down and keeps track of prices on paper or using an online paper trading portfolio service. For example, if the trader sees that IBM is trading within a narrow range, but expects it to break out higher or lower, he or she would write down the current market price and follow it over time to see if that assumption is correct.

Using the tools and information from the first four chapters, the reader now wants to look for actual trading situations and begin paper trading (templates for paper trading specific option strategies are located in the Appendix). Looking through finance-related web sites such as Optionetics.com, Bloomberg.com, and the Interactive Wall Street Journal, or newspapers such as the business section of the *New York Times* will provide a reader with examples of stocks that have been making the headlines and, therefore, exhibiting relatively high levels of volatility. Once the trader has found a dozen or so of these stocks, creating charts and applying indicators can provide a sense of the price action and volatility of each stock. Statistical volatility should also be charted. Unfortunately, there are no free sources to date that provide statistical volatility information. It must either be computed or found using a pay service such as Optionetics.com Platinum (check out the two-week FREE trial membership).

Now the trader wants to ask a series of questions. For example: Has there been an overreaction? Is the price of the stock responding in a reasonable manner? Has volatility fallen well outside of its normal range? Is there likely to be a reversion to the mean and, if so, how long will it take? All of these questions, of course, are not easy to answer, and the trader must therefore use all of the tools available at his or her disposal. This process includes looking at statistical volatility over different time frames, analyzing both short-term and long-term charts, and applying indicators such as Bollinger bands, ATR, and moving averages. Once an attractive situation appears to have materialized, the next step is to note the current price of the stock or index, set a price target, specify a time frame for the stock to move to this target (3, 6, 12, etc. months), and then monitor the price changes in a journal.

Vocabulary List

Please define the following terms:

- Breakout
- Buy signals
- Gap down
- Gap up
- Moving average
- Normal range
- Overbought condition
- Oversold condition
- Price consolidation
- Resistance
- Reversion to the mean
- Sell signals
- Spike
- Support
- True Range

5

The World of Stock Options

Summary

Trading stock options has been the most rewarding part of our professional trading careers. Through the years, we have traded stocks, commodities, and futures, but none come close to giving us the personal and financial satisfaction we attain from trading options. Some find it hard to believe. In fact, stock options are often considered risky investments and the domain of only speculators. That is not necessarily true. We are not all speculators. Those of us with managed risk experience use options to create a number of different risk/reward situations. Consider some of the objectives an option strategist can achieve:

- Generate an income stream.
- Protect an existing stock position.
- Position a trade to profit on a big swing in a stock, regardless of market direction.
- Profit from a move sideways in a stock.

To get the most out of options trading, however, a fundamental understanding of these derivatives is a must. Options can be used to create almost any type of risk/reward scenario fathomable. When used incorrectly, however, options can cause financial disaster. The strategist must have a clear understanding of the basics—the difference between a put and a call, what the strike price represents, and when the option expires—as well as the more complex aspects of options trading like what happens to an option when volatility falls, what is the potential loss from selling a naked call, and what happens if an option is assigned? After reading Chapter 5 of *The Volatility Course*, the reader should understand:

- The difference between a put and a call.
- The main determinants of an option's price.
- How to find an option quote.
- How an option pricing model is used to solve for both an option's price as well as its volatility.
- The roles of the various stock exchanges.
- The function of the Options Clearing Corporation.
- The role of the brokerage firms when it comes to options trading.

As of this writing, the options market includes five different U.S. exchanges with more than 725 million listed option contracts. It is a vibrant market full of trading opportunities. In addition, there are almost an unlimited number of ways to use options and structure trades to profit in a variety of situations. While most novice traders begin trading by aggressively buying calls on stocks that they expect to go up, that is a simple and sometimes foolhardy approach to the market. After almost 10 years as investment seminar speakers, we have heard countless tales of how options have destroyed individual trading accounts. In short, while there are many ways to use options, attempting to get rich quick is not a prudent approach. Using options for the sole purpose of speculation often results in financial losses. Instead, it is important to consider the versatility of options and how they can be used to create countless trading strategies with a wide array of risk/reward potentials.

Questions and Exercises

1. True or False: Options traders are more concerned with historical volatility than implied volatility.
2. Name five things you can do using options as a trading instrument.
   1. ______________________________
   2. ______________________________
   3. ______________________________
   4. ______________________________
   5. ______________________________
3. Why are options called derivatives?

   ____

   ____
4. Option prices on a high volatility stock will be ____________ than the equivalent option (with the same price) on a low volatility stock.

   A. Lower

   B. Higher

5. True or False: Options offer opportunities to make profits regardless of whether the stock or index moves in either direction.

6. In 1973, the ____________ formalized the trading of option contracts.
   A. Securities and Exchange Commission (SEC)
   B. Chicago Board Options Exchange (CBOE)
   C. Commodity Futures Trading Commission (CFTC)
   D. Options Clearing Corporation (OCC)

7. The option contract specifies a price, known as the ____________, at which the stock can be bought or sold and a fixed date, called the ____________, by which the transaction must take place.
   A. Strike price/Expiration date
   B. Premium/Reversion date
   C. Bid/Assignment date

8. When puts and calls trade on one of the organized exchanges, they are referred to as ____________.
   A. Listed options
   B. Organized options
   C. Exchange options
   D. Underlying options
   E. Security options

9. True or False: The seller of an option is also known as a "writer."

10. True or False: Option buyers must hold the option until it expires.

11. True or False: There is no difference between American- and European-style options.

12. The call option gives the owner (the holder or buyer) the right to ____________ the underlying security at a specific price during a specific period of time.
    A. Buy
    B. Sell

13. The put option gives the owner the right to ____________ a specific stock (underlying asset) at a specific price over a predetermined period of time.
    A. Buy
    B. Sell

14. True or False: If a call is assigned and exercised, the call writer is obligated to deliver 100 shares of the underlying stock to the option buyer at the strike price.

15. True or False: If a put is assigned and exercised, the put writer is obligated to buy 100 shares of the underlying stock from the option buyer at the strike price.

16. An in-the-money call option has a strike price ____________ the stock price.

    A. Above

    B. Below

    C. The same as

17. An out-of-the-money put option has a strike price ____________ the stock price.

    A. Above

    B. Below

    C. The same as

18. Any option contract can be discussed in terms of specifications regarding ____________.

    A. The type (put or call)

    B. The underlying stock or index (e.g., IBM or QQQ)

    C. The strike price

    D. The expiration month

    E. All of the above

19. Each stock is assigned to one of three quarterly expiration cycles. Name the months in these cycles.

    Cycle 1: ____

    Cycle 2: ____

    Cycle 3: ____

20. True or False: Expiration occurs on the first Saturday of the expiration month.

21. The ____________ of the underlying asset is the most important factor in determining the value of an option.

    A. Fundamentals

    B. Popularity

    C. Price

    D. Historical volatility

    E. Implied volatility

22. Why are options referred to as "wasting assets"?

    ____

    ____

23. True or False: Moneyness describes the relationship between the price of an underlying asset and the price of an option on that same underlying asset.

24. The difference between the strike price and the underlying asset's price is known as ____________.
    A. Time value
    B. Extrinsic value
    C. Intrinsic value
25. True or False: At-the-money (ATM) options and out-of-the-money (OTM) options have zero intrinsic value.
26. The ____________ is the safety net behind the options market and ensures that investors are not at risk of a financial collapse on the part of a broker, an exchange, or other options market participant.
    A. Securities and Exchange Commission (SEC)
    B. International Securities Exchange (ISE)
    C. Options Clearing Corporation (OCC)
    D. National Association of Securities Dealers (NASD)
27. True or False: An option with only three weeks remaining in its life will see a much faster rate of time decay than an equivalent option with 12 months of life remaining.
28. Name five things that influence an option's premium.
    1. ____________________
    2. ____________________
    3. ____________________
    4. ____________________
    5. ____________________
29. True or False: The higher the volatility of the underlying asset, the higher the option premium.
30. True or False: The theoretical value of an option derived from any option pricing model will not always be equal to its value in the marketplace.
31. If open interest on the August IBM 75 call is 3,020, what does this mean?
    ____
    ____
32. True or False: In order to trade options, all you have to do is open a brokerage account.
33. True or False: Index options settle for cash, and not shares.

Media Assignment

Up until this chapter, options have not been specifically discussed. Now, however, the reader wants to turn his or her attention to the fascinating world of options trading. A solid understanding of the basics—such as the difference between puts and calls, time decay, and implied volatility (IV)—are paramount to trading success. In that respect, there are a number of different web sites that offer educational materials for the student of options. Three to consider as starting points are the Chicago Board Options Exchange (www.cboe.com), the Options Clearing Corporation (www.optionsclearing.com), and Optionetics.com (www.optionetics.com). An appropriate textbook for learning about options is *The Options Strategist* by Larry McMillan. The books *Trade Options Online* and *The Options Course* (both by George Fontanills) are also great places to learn the details of options trading in today's market.

In addition to developing an understanding of and appreciation for the options market, the reader also needs to find the tools for computing implied volatility of any option. Some web sites, such as that of the Chicago Board Options Exchange, offer option pricing calculators that can be used to compute implied volatility. Many options trading software packages also provide the tools necessary for computing implied volatility. Additionally, some brokerage firms, such as Thinkorswim.com, provide analytical tools for studying options. Before opening an account with a broker, it is worthwhile to examine what sort of options trading tools the firm provides. Some will offer implied volatility information, but most do not. Finally, pay services, such as Optionetics.com Platinum and ivolatility.com, can provide present and past implied volatility information.

Regardless of the source, to trade volatility successfully the options trader will need access to both implied and historical volatility information. The media assignments from the past two chapters were designed to help the reader become adept at stock charts and identifying sources of statistical volatility information for a stock or an index. Implied volatility is the next piece of the puzzle. Again, select a dozen or so stocks that have recently experienced volatility for one reason or another. Looking through the headlines from the financial press will help in this endeavor. Now, find the options and option symbols for the stocks in question. Examine implied volatility. Is it high or low? How does it compare to statistical volatility? Most often, implied volatility will be greater than statistical volatility, but not always. If implied volatility is low relative to statistical volatility and past levels of IV, the options are cheap. On the other hand, if implied volatility is high relative to past IV and to the stock's statistical volatility, options are expensive. Enter your findings in your trading journal.

Vocabulary List

Please define the following terms:

- American-style options
- Assignment
- At-the-money (ATM)
- Black-Scholes model
- Call
- Closing transaction
- Derivative
- Dividends
- Downside move
- European-style options

- Exercise
- Expiration
- Implied volatility
- In-the-money (ITM)
- Intrinsic value
- LEAPS
- Opening transaction
- Open interest
- Options Clearing Corporation (OCC)
- Out-of-the-money (OTM)
- Put
- Time decay
- Time value
- Underlying asset (security)
- Wasting assets
- Writer

6

Implied Volatility

Summary

Options are derivative instruments; so their values are derived from other assets. Most traders understand that an important factor in determining the value of a stock option is the price of underlying stock. Therefore, if they expect a stock to go up, they might buy calls. However, while the price of the underlying asset is an important determinant of an option's value, there are others. Many traders do not give enough attention to the other factors that influence the price of an option. For example, time decay is extremely important in considering the value of an option over time. Financial losses often occur when traders do not fully understand that options, unlike stocks, gradually diminish in value until the time that they expire. The phenomenon is known as time decay.

Implied volatility (IV) is another factor. Implied volatility is a determinant of an option's value that can change instantaneously. The CBOE Volatility Index is an example of implied volatility. It measures the implied volatility of OEX options. Quotes are available throughout the day under the ticker symbol VIX. After a major news event (earnings, shortfall, Fed rate decision, military conflict, etc.) that drives stocks sharply lower, VIX will spike higher to reflect rising implied volatility in the options market. An example occurred in late July 2002 when WorldCom said it had misstated financial results and VIX, which normally fluctuates between 20% and 30%, surged toward the 60% level.

Implied volatility of an option can change over time and as the demand for an option rises and falls. For that reason, IV is an important guide for the option strategist—it tells whether an option is cheap or expensive. Consequently, implied volatility also dictates whether the strategist is best served by being a buyer or a seller of that option. Finally, changes in implied volatility can be a reason why an option fails to increase in value even though the speculator correctly predicted the direction of the stock. In fact, implied volatility is such an important factor to understand that Chapter 6 of *The Volatility Course* was dedicated entirely to the topic.

In order to find the implied volatility of an option, the strategist must use an options pricing model like the one developed by Fischer Black and Myron Scholes in 1973. The model is used to determine what volatility the market is implying in an option contract (thus the term *implied volatility*). When doing so, a number of inputs are required:

- The stock price.
- The strike price of the option.
- The option price.
- The time remaining until expiration.
- The prevailing interest rate.
- In certain circumstances, any dividends paid by the stock.

All of these factors have an influence on the option price. When the option premium increases but the other factors stay the same, the change in price is due to a change in implied volatility. In contrast to historical volatility, which is a measure of past prices, implied volatility reflects expectations regarding the stock or market's future volatility. Therefore, the options trader can learn a great deal about a stock's volatility by looking at both implied and historical volatility together.

Questions and Exercises

1. Implied volatility is expressed as a percentage and is derived by using _________.
   A. Past prices
   B. Open interest
   C. Volume
   D. An options pricing model
   E. None of the above

2. True or False: Implied volatility indicates to the option strategist whether options are cheap or expensive.

3. When two options on the same stock have vastly different implied volatilities, it is known as volatility ____________.
   A. Signal
   B. Leverage
   C. Opportunity
   D. Skew
   E. Disaster

4. True or False: Volatility never changes, and remains the same over time.

5. Name three things that impact implied volatility.
   1. ______________________________
   2. ______________________________
   3. ______________________________

6. True or False: When implied volatility rises, options become cheap; when implied volatility falls, the option premiums rise.

7. Dividends are periodic payments a company makes to its ____________.
   A. Employees
   B. Owners
   C. Friends and relatives
   D. Shareholders
   E. Venture capitalists

8. True or False: The impact of dividends will not be equal on all call options.

9. Implied volatility gives a sense of what traders and market makers believe the volatility of the stock will be in the ____________.
   A. Future
   B. Past
   C. Future or the past
   D. Stock market
   E. None of the above

10. True or False: In the case of a takeover rumor, the call options generally see growing investor interest and, as a result, the implied volatility will rise.

11. True or False: Higher interest rates mean lower option prices, while lower interest rates mean higher premiums.

12. The first step in determining whether options are cheap or expensive is to compare ____________.
    A. Historical volatility to implied volatility
    B. Implied volatility over time
    C. Implied volatility to Bollinger bands
    D. Implied volatility to ATR

13. CBOE Volatility Index, or VIX, provides real-time information regarding the implied volatility of ____________.
    A. QQQ options
    B. QVN options
    C. S&P 500 index options
    D. S&P 100 (OEX) index options

14. If the theoretical value of an option is computed using the statistical volatility of the stock equal to 15%, but the implied volatility of the option is 25%, the market price of the option will be __________________ the theoretical value.

    A. Lower than

    B. Higher than

    C. The same as

15. The protective put provides ____________ on a long stock position just in case the stock takes a dive.

    A. Support

    B. Resistance

    C. Time decay

    D. Insurance

    E. Leverage

16. True or False: When stock prices are falling, implied volatility tends to rise; but when stock prices are rising, implied volatility tends to fall.

17. The covered call is also known as a ____________.

    A. Vertical spread

    B. Long position

    C. Hedge

    D. Spread

    E. Buy-write

18. In a covered call, one call is sold for every ____________ shares of stock that are held.

    A. 2,000

    B. 1,000

    C. 500

    D. 100

    E. 50

19. True or False: In the covered call strategy, the owner of stock is also a seller, or writer, of calls.

20. True or False: The covered call is best used when the investor is moderately bearish on a stock.

21. Calculate the maximum risk and reward as well as the breakeven for each of the following trades:

Protective Put: Buy 100 Shares XYZ @ 40.00 and Buy 1 Oct XYZ 40 Put @ 4

Maximum Reward = ______________________________

Maximum Risk = ______________________________

Breakeven = ______________________________

Covered Call: Buy 100 Shares XYZ @ 37.50 and Sell 1 Oct XYZ 40 Call @ 3

Maximum Reward = ______________________________

Maximum Risk = ______________________________

Breakeven = ______________________________

Strategy Reviews

Protective Put

Strategy = Buy the underlying security and buy an ATM or OTM put option.

Market Opportunity = Seeks to profit from an increase in the value of the underlying asset, but uses the put as protection in case of a decline.

Maximum Risk = Limited to stock price minus the strike price plus the price paid for the put option premium.

Maximum Profit = Unlimited as the stock moves higher.

Breakeven = Stock price + put option premium.

Margin = 50% of the stock and no margin for the long put.

Covered Call

Strategy = Buy the underlying security and sell an OTM call option.

Market Opportunity = Look for a bullish to neutral market where a slow rise in the price of the underlying asset is anticipated with little risk of decline.

Maximum Risk = Limited to the downside as the underlying stock falls below the breakeven all the way to zero.

Maximum Profit = Limited to the credit received from the short call option + (short call strike price – price of long underlying asset) times value per point.

Breakeven = Price of the underlying asset at initiation – short call premium received.

Margin = Required. Amount subject to broker's discretion.

Media Assignment

In the preceding chapter, the reader was encouraged to find a source of implied volatility information. One common method for computing implied volatility is by using options pricing calculators that are found on a number of web sites and in many options trading software packages. In addition, some brokerage firms allow account holders to view options-related research, which sometimes includes implied volatility. Another place to find option information is Optionetics.com. This includes the subscription-based Platinum site, as well as the free ranker that is accessible from the home page. The ranker, in turn, can provide lists of options that are cheap (low implied volatility) or expensive (high implied volatility).

The next media assignment incorporates the information from the past two chapters. Specifically, the reader now wants to paper trade (as described in Chapter 4) using the paper trading templates in the Appendix. In the protective put strategy, the first step is to use the Optionetics.com ranker to identify half a dozen stocks that have cheap options. Next, look over the stock charts and attempt to identify the ones that appear overbought using the indicators described in earlier chapters—Bollinger bands, moving averages, and so on. Search the financial headlines for potential signs of trouble or a pending earnings announcement. Set a price target and time frame for the stock to move lower. Now, looking through the options chain for the stock, find an at-the-money or near-the-money option that expires one or two months after your target date. For example, if you believe the stock will fall by the middle of October, find the put that expires in November or December. Make a note of the stock and the option prices (bids and offers). Revisit the trade in mid-October and document the results. Since the time decay is greatest in the option's final month, it makes sense to close the position, or roll over to longer-term puts, no less than 30 days prior to expiration. The idea is to understand how the put can help or protect the underlying stock in the event of a stock decline.

Repeat the process using expensive options and the covered call strategy. Namely, use the ranker available on the Optionetics.com home page and identify stocks with expensive options. Look for signs that the stock is oversold or ready to reverse. Search through the financial headlines for possible reasons the stock might move higher. Now set a time frame and price target for the stock. Look for an option that has a strike price at or slightly above your price objective and that expires within the time frame you set as a target. In the case of the covered call, time decay is working in favor of the position, and therefore it is okay to hold the option until expiration. Use the paper trading templates in the Appendix to track the trades to completion.

Vocabulary List

Please define the following terms:

- Buy-write
- CBOE Volatility Index (VIX)
- Covered call
- Delta
- Gamma
- The greeks
- Hedge
- Implied volatility
- Leverage
- Protective put
- Skew
- Stock split
- Theta
- Vega

7

VIX and Other Sentiment Indicators

Summary

Sentiment analysis is the process of studying the prevailing market psychology. It is an ongoing effort in determining whether investors are primarily bullish or bearish. Sentiment analysis also involves the art of contrary thinking. That is, it requires the assumption that the general investment public is usually wrong at major turning points in the market. When the public, or the crowd as it is sometimes called, is optimistic or bullish on the market, the contrary thinker will take a negative or bearish stance toward the market; however, when the prevailing psychology is overly bearish or pessimistic toward the stock market, the contrarian will develop a more bullish stance toward stocks.

There are several tools available for studying market psychology. Some are more subjective and examine sentiment by looking at the financial headlines, the talk from Wall Street analysts, or investment-related publications. Other measures of market sentiment are more quantitative in nature. For example, there are a number of tools that are indigenous to the options market that gauge sentiment, such as put-to-call ratios and the CBOE Volatility Index, or VIX. Surveys of newsletter writers, levels of short interest, the market for initial public offerings, and margin debt also provide gauges of market psychology.

Sentiment analysis is also a search for extremes. In attempting to pinpoint major turning points in the stock market, it is not enough to identify periods when the crowd is moderately bullish or somewhat bearish. Instead, the contrarian is searching for extremely high levels of optimism or pessimism to indicate that the market is ready to turn. It is only when the majority of investors are on one side of the market (bullish or bearish) does it pay to take on a contrarian approach. In fact, there is an adage on Wall Street that says the crowd is usually "right on the trend, but wrong on both ends."

Questions and Exercises

1. ____________ different exchanges list options.

   A. Two

   B. Three

   C. Five

   D. Seven

   E. Ten

2. True or False: When the mood toward stocks and the market turns pessimistic, most investors will lean toward caution and buy put options for downside protection.

3. When investors turn optimistic regarding stocks and the U.S. market, speculative activity will lead to ____________ in call buying.

   A. An increase

   B. A decrease

4. Looking at the options market to glean information about investor psychology is also known as ____________.

   A. Fundamental analysis

   B. Technical analysis

   C. Sentiment analysis

   D. Broad market analysis

5. True or False: When the crowd is predominantly pessimistic regarding the market, the contrarian will become optimistic.

6. The key to using sentiment analysis successfully lies in identifying ____________.

   A. Trends

   B. Volatility

   C. Extremes

   D. Bear markets

   E. Bull markets

7. ____________ has become the number one gauge of market volatility available today.

   A. The put/call ratio

   B. The Dow

   C. VIX

   D. VXN

8. During times of uncertainty and market turmoil, VIX will ____________ to reflect greater expectations regarding future volatility.

   A. Rise

   B. Fall

   C. Remain the same

   D. Fluctuate

9. VIX is often referred to as ____________.

   A. A buy signal

   B. A sell signal

   C. Sentiment analysis indicator

   D. The fear gauge

10. True or False: During the market crash in October 1987, VIX hit a record high of 173%, which has since been surpassed only by the mini-crash of 1989.

11. True or False: S&P 500 index options and Dow Jones Industrial Average index options settle European-style.

12. The proliferation of a large number of ____________ has been the most important factor behind the drop in OEX option trading.

    A. High-technology stocks with available options

    B. Requirements for options trading

    C. Losses by experienced investors

    D. Other index option contracts

13. True or False: VXN was created to track the implied volatility of the popular NDX options contract.

14. True or False: The VIX and VXN tend to move in opposite directions most of the time.

15. Match the index options to the correct ticker symbol in Table 7.1.

Table 7.1 Match Index Option to Ticker Symbol

Index	*Tickers*
Nasdaq 100 Index Trust	OEX
Mini-Nasdaq 100	SPX
S&P 100 Index	DJX
S&P 500 Index	QQQ
Dow Jones Industrial Average	MNX

16. The ____________ is a composite measure of implied volatility on QQQ options.

    A. MNX

    B. QQV

    C. VXN

    D. VIX

17. Name two differences between the MNX and the QQQ.

    1. ____

    2. ____

18. True or False: VIX, VXN, and QQV tend to rise when investors become complacent toward the outlook for the market and expect volatility to fall.

19. A high VIX means ____________ stocks (not options); but a low VIX urges ____________.

    A. Buy/Selling

    B. Sell/Caution

    C. Buy/Caution

    D. Sell/Buying

20. True or False: It is rare to see VIX dip below the historical volatility of the OEX.

21. True or False: Most option traders are either hedgers or speculators, and their strategies are limited to the straight purchase of puts and calls.

22. One of the put/call ratios more widely used by traders today is computed as the total volume of puts divided by the total volume of calls on the ____________.

    A. Chicago Board Options Exchange

    B. Nasdaq

    C. American Stock Exchange

    D. New York Stock Exchange

23. When the CBOE put-to-call ratio rises toward the high end or above 1.00—as it did in the fall of 1998, right before the market hit bottom—traders should become alert for ____________.

    A. Selling opportunities

    B. Buying opportunities

    C. Range-trading opportunities

24. When stocks fall, put buying ____________; when stocks leap forward, call activity ____________.
    A. Stops/Drops
    B. Rises/Increases
    C. Rises/Decreases
    D. Decreases/Increases
    E. Decreases/Remains the same

25. True or False: When the CBOE put-to-call ratio rises toward the high end or above 1.00, it is a sign of excessive market pessimism and heavy put buying.

Media Assignment

The following media assignment is designed to help the reader get in tune with the prevailing market psychology. Two of the most important tools indigenous to the options market—the CBOE put-to-call ratio and the CBOE Volatility Index—can help the reader to gauge market sentiment. Because the activity in the options market reflects the actual trading decisions of millions of investors, these indicators provide a view into what investors are doing with real money. The fact is, most option traders are betting on the direction of the stock or the market through the purchase of puts and calls. As the buying and selling take place, sometimes emotions become strong and the crowd often takes on characteristics similar to a mob. When these emotions reach extremes of fear and greed, profit opportunities arise for the savvy trader, or to the contrarian who is willing to bet against the crowd. Sentiment analysis is the art of identifying the extremes.

One of the most reliable gauges of investor sentiment is the CBOE put-to-call ratio. It equals the total number of puts divided by the number of calls traded on the Chicago Board Options Exchange. During times when traders turn excessively bullish, the number of calls traded will increase relative to the number of puts. Most often, there is more call than put buying when dealing with stock options. For that reason, the total CBOE put/call ratio is usually less than 1.00. When excessive levels of optimism exist, the total CBOE put/call ratio will fall below 0.50. When traders turn bearish, the ratio will spike above 1.00. Again, when looking for extremes, the trader looks for high put/call ratios to signal a market bottom and low numbers to signal a top. The ratio is posted at the close of each trading session on the Chicago Board Options Exchange web site and should be recorded on a regular basis for this media assignment.

The CBOE Volatility Index, or VIX, is the market's "fear gauge." It is a measure of implied volatility on S&P 100 (OEX) options. During times of market volatility, investors will buy OEX put options as a hedge or protection. The aggressive buying of OEX puts, in turn, leads to a surge in implied volatility and a rise in VIX. Therefore, when VIX rises, it is a sign of investor angst. In contrast, when VIX falls to low levels, it suggests investor bullishness or complacency. Therefore, when the volatility index falls at the low end of its recent trading range (18–23%), traders should turn cautious. When VIX spikes to the upper end of its recent trading range

(35–40%), the strategist can take it as a signal that market fear has become exaggerated and can consequently assume selling has been overdone.

The trading range for VIX will change through time, however, and for the purpose of this media assignment the reader wants to chart the recent trends with respect to this indicator. To do so, simply visit Optionetics.com and create a chart of the Volatility Index using the ticker symbol $VIX. Additionally, create an overlay chart that includes both VIX and the S&P 100 (symbol $OEX). Notice how the OEX often moves lower when VIX begins moving off of the lower end of its trading range. Also notice that major bottoms in the OEX often coincide with spikes in VIX.

In addition to viewing market psychology through put-to-call ratios and VIX, the trader also wants to stay in touch with the prevailing market psychology reflected in comments from the financial press. For example, cover stories of major magazines often turn extremely negative and bleak regarding the outlook for the stock market just as the bear market is reaching an end. Also, pay attention to the pundits and market gurus. When they are predominantly bullish on the market, it could be a sign that stocks are ready to head lower. In addition, Investors Intelligence, Market Vane, and the American Association of Individual Investors publish weekly surveys of investor sentiment. The latest readings can be found in *Barron's*. Finally, for a weekly discussion of the sentiment picture, visit the free articles at Optionetics.com and look for a column entitled "Sentiment Journal" posted every Friday afternoon. As always, keep a journal of your findings and how they relate to your paper trades.

Vocabulary List

Please define the following terms:

- Contrarian
- DJX
- Extremes
- Market bottom
- Market top
- MNX
- Nasdaq 100 (NDX)
- OEX
- Put/call ratio
- QQQ
- QQV
- S&P 500 (SPX)
- Sentiment analysis
- Speculative activity
- VIX
- VXN

8

Exploiting Low Volatility

Summary

Implied volatility (IV) is one of the most important principles for option traders to understand. Unfortunately, many option traders overlook it and end up losing money due to a lack of understanding. Nevertheless, as we have seen from earlier chapters, IV measures the amount by which an underlying asset is expected to fluctuate in the future. Implied volatility also gauges the speed of change with respect to a stock or an index. Stocks that experience large and rapid price changes will often command option premiums with higher levels of implied volatility.

Put differently, implied volatility is sometimes considered a measure of market confusion. The more confused a market is, the better chance an option has of ending up in-the-money (ITM)—because a violent market moves very rapidly, while a stable market moves slowly. Option prices and implied volatility will reflect the confusion or volatility associated with a stock or market. All else being equal, the more violent and rapid the market, the more expensive (the higher the IV) the options contract. Intuitively, this makes sense. After all, if an option has a greater chance of moving in-the-money, the option premium will be higher. Option buyers will be willing to pay a higher price for an option that has a greater potential for moving ITM prior to expiration.

The option trader wants to consider the volatility of each stock individually and search for extremes. Doing so will enable the trader to take advantage of a variety of different trading scenarios. Specifically, knowing whether an option is exhibiting high or low levels of volatility will dictate what trading strategy to implement. This chapter explores trading strategies that are best positioned to make money when volatility is low. It is basically an effort to find situations with little confusion and where most market participants do not expect the stock or market to make a significant move higher or lower. As a result, the implied volatility will be low to reflect those expectations.

The first step in trading low IV is to define what constitutes low volatility. One way to consider implied volatility is to compare the option's IV to the historical volatility of the stock. Another way is to look at an implied volatility chart and determine if current levels of IV are high or low relative to past levels of IV. When IV is relatively low compared to either statistical volatility or past levels of IV, it could be a sign that options are cheap. Of course, the true test is whether the current levels of implied volatility are low relative to both the underlying asset's statistical volatility and past levels of IV. If so, the strategies in this chapter are appropriate.

An understanding of reversion to the mean is essential to trading low volatility. In a nutshell, if the volatility has been lower than normal for a period of time, the odds say that it will eventually revert to its mean, or average, and begin to move higher. If so, there are certain strategies that will benefit if IV does indeed climb higher. Simple strategies like the long call and the long put are examples of strategies that benefit from increasing levels of implied volatility. Of course, the direction of the underlying asset is more important than changes in IV when the strategist is simply buying puts and calls. Nevertheless, long calls and long puts are discussed as the first strategies designed to profit in a low implied volatility environment, and each example paves the way for the straddle—our first complex strategy. The straddle involves the purchase of both puts and calls, and also stands to gain from rising IV. From there, the reader will be introduced to debit spreads and ratio backspreads. In sum, the essence of this chapter is to provide readers with a variety of different strategies to employ when (1) implied volatility is low, and (2) the trader expects a reversion to the mean.

Questions and Exercises

1. If implied volatility is high, an option appears ____________.
   A. Cheap
   B. Expensive
   C. Illiquid
   D. None of the above
2. The more confused a market is, the better chance an option has of ending up ____________.
   A. In-the-money
   B. At-the-money
   C. Out-of-the-money
3. The maximum risk of buying a call is limited to the ____________.
   A. Strike price × 100
   B. Strike price – call premium
   C. Underlying stock price – strike price
   D. Call premium × 100

4. The long call is ____________ when the price of the underlying asset rises above the strike price of the call.

   A. In-the-money

   B. At-the-money

   C. Out-of-the-money

   D. Near-the-money

5. Fill in the blanks in the candlestick diagram in Figure 8.1 using the terms in the adjacent box (some words are used twice).

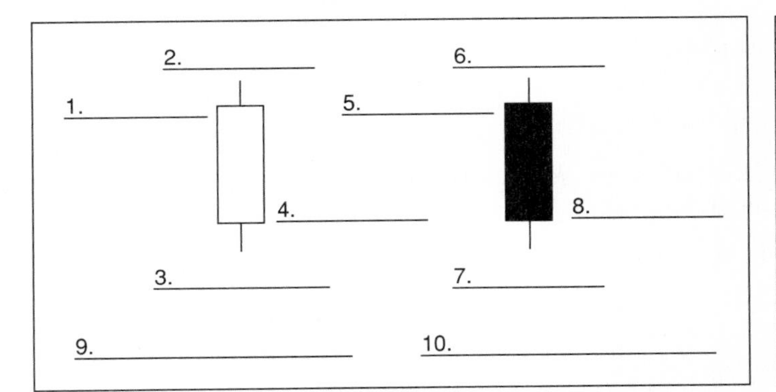

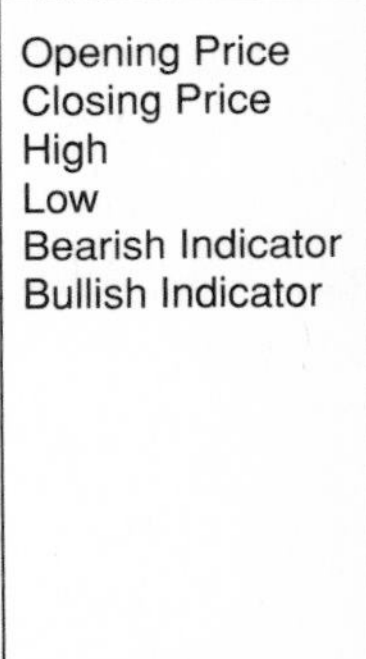

Figure 8.1 Candlestick Diagram

6. A call's premium will ____________ in value depending on how high the underlying instrument ____________ in price beyond the strike price of the call.

   A. Increase/Drops

   B. Decrease/Rises

   C. Increase/Rises

   D. Remains the same/Drops

   E. Drop/Increases

7. A strategist will go long a put option in anticipation that the stock or index will ____________.

   A. Rise

   B. Fall

   C. Remain the same

   D. None of the above

8. True or False: The premium of the long put option will show up as a credit in your trading account.

9. True or False: A put option is in-the-money (ITM) when the strike price is higher than the market price of the underlying asset.

10. True or False: The bear put spread involves the simultaneous purchase of a put option and sale of a put option, with different expiration dates, but the same strike prices.

11. When using the bull call spread, the strategist anticipates the stock or index to ____________.

    A. Rise

    B. Fall

    C. Remain the same

12. True or False: The bull call spread is more likely to feel a negative impact from falling IV than the bear put spread.

13. True or False: The call ratio backspread is a type of trade that is best used when implied volatility is low.

14. It is best to purchase straddles when implied volatility is ____________.

    A. High

    B. Low

    C. Unpredictable

    D. In a range

    E. Decreasing

15. True or False: Entry into either a call or put ratio backspread requires high levels of implied volatility.

16. Calculate the maximum reward and risk, as well as breakevens, for the following trades with XYZ trading at 40:

    Long Call: Long 1 Oct XYZ 40 Call @ 3

    Strategy = ____

    Maximum Reward = ______________________________________

    Maximum Risk = ____

    Breakeven = ____

    Long Put: Long 1 Oct XYZ 40 Put @ 2.50

    Strategy = ____

    Maximum Reward = ______________________________________

    Maximum Risk = ____

    Breakeven = ____

Straddle: Long 1 Oct XYZ 40 Call @ 3 and Long 1 Oct XYZ 40 Put @ 2.50

Strategy = ______________________________

Maximum Reward = ______________________________

Maximum Risk = ______________________________

Upside Breakeven = ______________________________

Downside Breakeven = ______________________________

Bear Put Spread: Long 1 Oct XYZ 45 Put @ 4 and Short 1 Oct XYZ 35 Put @ 1.25

Strategy = ______________________________

Maximum Reward = ______________________________

Maximum Risk = ______________________________

Breakeven = ______________________________

Bull Call Spread: Long 1 Oct XYZ 35 Call @ 5 and Short 1 Oct XYZ 45 Call @ 1.50

Strategy = ______________________________

Maximum Reward = ______________________________

Maximum Risk = ______________________________

Breakeven = ______________________________

Call Ratio Backspread: Short 2 Oct XYZ 35 Calls @ 5 and Long 3 Oct XYZ 40 Calls @ 3

Strategy = ______________________________

Net Credit = ______________________________

Maximum Reward = ______________________________

Maximum Risk = ______________________________

Upside Breakeven = ______________________________

Downside Breakeven = ______________________________

Put Ratio Backspread: Short 2 Oct XYZ 40 Puts @ 2.50 and Long 3 Oct XYZ 35 Puts @ 1.25

Strategy = ______________________________

Net Credit = ______________________________

Maximum Reward = ______________________________

Maximum Risk = ______________________________

Upside Breakeven = ______________________________

Downside Breakeven = ______________________________

Strategy Reviews

Long Call

Strategy = Buy a call option.

Market Opportunity = Look for a bullish market where a rise above the breakeven is anticipated.

Maximum Risk = Limited to the amount paid for the call.

Maximum Profit = Unlimited as the price of the underlying instrument rises above the breakeven.

Breakeven = Call strike price + call premium.

Margin = None.

Long Put

Strategy = Buy a put option.

Market Opportunity = Look for a bearish market where you anticipate a fall in the price of the underlying below the breakeven.

Maximum Risk = Limited to the price paid for the put option premium.

Maximum Profit = Limited as the stock price falls below the breakeven to zero.

Breakeven = Put strike price – put premium.

Margin = None.

Long Straddle

Strategy = Purchase an ATM call and an ATM put with the same strike price and the same expiration.

Market Opportunity = Look for a market with low implied volatility options where a sharp volatility increase is anticipated.

Maximum Risk = Limited to the net debit paid.

Maximum Profit = Unlimited to the upside and limited to the downside as the stock falls to zero. Profit requires sufficient market movement but does not depend on market direction.

Upside Breakeven = ATM strike price + net debit paid.

Downside Breakeven = ATM strike price – net debit paid.

Margin = None.

Bear Put Spread

Strategy = Buy a higher strike put and sell a lower strike put with the same expiration date.

Market Opportunity = Look for a bearish market where you anticipate a modest decrease in the price of the underlying asset below the strike price of the short put option.

Maximum Risk = Limited to the net debit paid.

Maximum Profit = Limited [(difference in strike prices × 100) – net debit paid].

Breakeven = Higher put strike price – net debit paid.

Margin = Required. Amount subject to broker's discretion.

Bull Call Spread

Strategy = Buy a lower strike call and sell a higher strike call with the same expiration dates.

Market Opportunity = Look for a bullish market where you anticipate a modest increase in the price of the underlying above the price of the short call option.

Maximum Risk = Limited to the net debit paid for the spread.

Maximum Profit = Limited [(difference in strike prices × 100) – net debit paid].

Breakeven = Lower call strike price + net debit paid.

Margin = Required. Amount subject to broker's discretion—should be limited to the net debit on the trade.

Call Ratio Backspread

Strategy = Sell lower strike calls and buy a greater number of higher strike calls (the ratio must be less than $^2/_3$).

Market Opportunity = Look for a market where you anticipate a sharp rise with increasing volatility; place as a credit or at even.

Maximum Risk = Limited (# short calls × difference in strike prices) × 100 – net credit (or + net debit).

Maximum Profit = Unlimited above the upside breakeven and limited to the net credit below the downside breakeven.

Upside Breakeven = Higher strike call + [(difference in strike prices × # short calls)/(# long calls – # short calls)] – net credit (or + net debit).

Downside Breakeven = Strike price of the short call + net credit (or - net debit).

Margin = Required. Amount subject to broker's discretion.

Put Ratio Backspread

Strategy = Sell higher strike puts and buy a greater number of lower strike puts with a ratio less than $^{2}/_{3}$.

Market Opportunity = Look for a market where you anticipate a sharp decline with increased volatility; place as a credit or at even.

Maximum Risk = Limited (# short puts × difference in strike prices) × 100 – net credit (or + net debit).

Maximum Profit = Limited below the downside breakeven as the stock falls to zero and limited to the net credit above the upside breakeven.

Upside Breakeven = Higher strike put – net credit (or + net debit).

Downside Breakeven = Lower strike price – [(# short puts × difference in strikes)/(# long puts – # short puts)] + net credit (or – net debit).

Margin = Required. Amount subject to broker's discretion.

Media Assignment

In this media assignment, and throughout the rest of the book, the reader is encouraged to practice volatility trading by paper trading the market. Since most successful traders develop a repertoire of different trading strategies, this chapter introduces a few key approaches. In Chapter 6, the reader was encouraged to look for candidates for covered calls and protective puts. Now, the goal is to identify trading opportunities when implied volatility is low. Again, a starting point is the free ranker provided on the Optionetics.com home page. In this case, the user is looking for options that are considered cheap, which is another way of saying the implied volatility is low.

Once the trader has identified half a dozen stocks with cheap options, a number of different paper trading strategies are possible. For example, the long call and long put are directional bets that also benefit from rising levels of IV. If the charts and indicators (such as Bollinger bands or moving averages) indicate that the stock is overbought, the trader can paper trade at-the-money or out-of-the-money puts. If so, set price targets for the stock, determine a reasonable time frame, note the current bids and offers for a slightly out-of-the-money put, and plan your exit in advance. Generally, we don't advocate simply buying puts, but for paper trading it can be useful for understanding how falling stock prices can cause changes in implied volatility.

A better strategy in a low IV situation is the straddle. The straddle is an example of a nondirectional strategy that can make money whether the stock moves higher or lower. It is best to purchase straddles when implied volatility is low. Once you find a low IV situation and are unsure whether the stock is set to make a significant move higher or lower, paper trade a straddle by noting the bids and offers for the at-the-money (or nearest-to-the-money) puts and calls. In general, when paper trading straddles you will use the offer as the basis for the trade because that is the price you will likely pay in the real world. Noting both the bids and offers, however, will give you a better sense of how option prices change as the paper trade progresses.

If the charts and indicators suggest that the stock is set to make a move in a specific direction, the bull call spread and the bear put spread can also yield profits in a low implied volatility environment. Debit spreads do not necessarily benefit from rising IV, and they often are hurt by falling IV. Therefore, it is best to establish them in a low IV situation. In addition, the last strategy covered in this chapter is the ratio backspread. It is also best suited for options with low levels of implied volatility. Once you have identified a stock with cheap (low IV) options and strong signs of a forthcoming move higher or lower, paper trade both debit spreads and backspreads using the paper trading templates in the Appendix.

Vocabulary List

Please define the following terms:

- Bear put spread
- Bull call spread
- Call ratio backspread
- Downside breakeven
- Go long
- Go short
- Japanese candlestick
- Long call
- Long put
- Low volatility
- Naked option
- Offset
- Options chain
- Put ratio backspread
- Risk graph
- Short call
- Short put
- Straddle
- Upside breakeven
- Vega

9

Exploiting High Volatility

Summary

In the stock market, investors are attracted to moving prices. Rarely does a stock that has been trading quietly and within a well-defined range make headlines. Instead, investors are interested in the movers, or the stocks that have experienced high levels of volatility. Thus, the media is partly responsible for investor interest in fast-moving stocks. After all, the financial press gets the attention of readers and other market watchers by reporting on sensational or unusual events. Investors, in turn, react to the news. When the media reports on a favorable development for a stock or the market, the natural instinct is to buy shares. In contrast, when the news is downbeat or negative and stock prices are falling, the crowd generally responds by selling shares. There is a tendency for investors to react collectively, like a herd, and cause exaggerated moves in the stock market.

When investors, traders, and the media react to unusual events, there is a tendency for market volatility to increase. Most often, volatility is associated with falling stock prices. However, volatility can rise when the market climbs higher as well. Anytime there is confusion, caused by emotions such as fear or greed, rational decision making can give way to impulse and to mob behavior. During those times, the impact can also be felt in the options market. It is generally manifested as an increase in option premiums and implied volatility.

In Chapter 8, the reader was presented with different trading opportunities that arise in a low implied volatility environment—straddles, debit spreads, and ratio backspreads. Now the attention turns to the opposite: high volatility strategies. In sum, there are a number of different strategies that can yield profits when implied volatility is high and then moves lower. Some, such as short calls and puts, are basic, but carry relatively large risks. Others, such as credit spreads and butterflies, while a bit more complex, are important tools for the volatility trader's repertoire.

The high volatility approaches discussed in this chapter are popular strategies that are relatively easy to understand and implement. By applying these strategies in high volatility markets, you can expect to get more reward with less risk. Remember that option premiums rise when uncertainty is high and investors are willing to pay more for protection. During those times, it makes sense to be an option seller, because it is better to be an insurance salesperson when everyone wants protection than when no one needs insurance. The premiums are higher, and the ability to keep some or all of the premiums is greater too.

Questions and Exercises

1. True or False: Markets trading at a very low level of volatility have a high probability of a large move occurring.
2. True or False: When volatility is at a very high level, a substantial probability exists for the contract to maintain a trading range.
3. VIX is a sentiment analysis indicator that measures ____________.
   A. Volatility
   B. The length of a trend
   C. Crowd psychology
   D. Trading ranges
   E. Peaks and valleys
4. True or False: When the VIX is high, it's time to buy volatility; when the VIX is low, it's time to sell volatility.
5. The ____________ is a popular option strategy in which one call is sold to create an open short position against 100 shares of stock already owned by the option seller.
   A. Call ratio backspread
   B. Bull call spread
   C. Bear put spread
   D. Covered call
   E. Naked put option
6. A ____________ is a put option where the writer of the contract does not have a short position in the underlying stock to cover the contract.
   A. Call ratio backspread
   B. Bull call spread
   C. Bear put spread
   D. Covered call
   E. Naked put option

7. Whether selling naked puts or naked calls, the maximum profit is equal to the ____________.
   - A. Strike price – option premium × 100
   - B. Stock price – strike price × 100
   - C. Strike price + option premium × 100
   - D. Stock price + strike price × 100
   - E. Premium received from the sale of the option
8. If you sell a naked put option, make sure it has less than ____________ days to expiration.
   - A. 15
   - B. 30
   - C. 45
   - D. 60
9. A deposit made by a trader with a clearinghouse to ensure that he or she will fulfill any financial obligations resulting from his or her trades is called ____________.
   - A. A credit
   - B. A debit
   - C. Margin
   - D. A margin call
   - E. Assignment
10. A broker's demand that a customer deposit additional funds to cover the price change of the underlying market in a trade is called a ____________.
    - A. Credit
    - B. Debit
    - C. Margin
    - D. Margin call
    - E. Margin requirement
11. The two types of credit spreads are ____________.
    - A. The bull call spread and the bear put spread.
    - B. The bull put spread and the bear call spread.
    - C. The calendar spread and the call ratio backspread.
    - D. The covered call and the naked put.
    - E. The bull put spread and the bull call spread.
12. True or False: A bull put spread involves selling a put with the strike price that is closest to the market value of the underlying asset (stock) and buying a lower strike put to hedge against unlimited risk.

13. True or False: If you are selling high probability at-the-money or out-of-the-money put spreads, you will want to keep the time to expiration as long as possible.

14. A bear call spread is created by ____________ a call with a higher strike price and ____________ a call with a lower strike price.
    A. Selling/Purchasing
    B. Purchasing/Selling
    C. Purchasing/Purchasing
    D. Selling/Selling
    E. Borrowing/Returning

15. True or False: In a forward volatility skew market, higher strike options have higher implied volatility and can be overpriced.

16. A reverse volatility skew is an excellent market scenario for which strategies?
    A. Bull put spread
    B. Bear call spread
    C. Call ratio backspread
    D. Put ratio backspread

17. The butterfly spread is a market neutral trade that can use ____________.
    A. Only calls
    B. Only puts
    C. All calls or all puts
    D. LEAPS
    E. None of the above

18. True or False: If a combination of both calls and puts is created, it is called a golden butterfly.

19. True or False: There are no strategies that can make money with a drop in volatility.

20. Calculate the maximum reward and risk, as well as breakevens, for the following trades with XYZ trading at 50:

    Covered Call: Long 100 shares XYZ @ 50 and Short 1 Aug XYZ 55 Call @ 2.50

    Strategy = ____________________________

    Maximum Reward = ____________________________

    Maximum Risk = ____________________________

    Breakeven = ____________________________

Short Put: Short 1 Aug XYZ 50 Put @ 4

Strategy = ______________________________

Maximum Reward = ______________________________

Maximum Risk = ______________________________

Breakeven = ______________________________

Bull Put Spread: Long 1 Sept XYZ 45 Put @ 2 and Short 1 Sept XYZ 50 Put @ 4

Strategy = ______________________________

Maximum Reward = ______________________________

Maximum Risk = ______________________________

Breakeven = ______________________________

Bear Call Spread: Long 1 Sept XYZ 55 Call @ 2.50 and Short 1 Sept XYZ 50 Call @ 5

Strategy = ______________________________

Maximum Reward = ______________________________

Maximum Risk = ______________________________

Breakeven = ______________________________

Iron Butterfly Spread: Long 1 Sept XYZ 55 Call @ 2.50, Short 1 Sept XYZ 50 Call @ 5, Short 1 Sept XYZ 45 Put @ 2, Long 1 Sept XYZ 40 Put @ 1

Strategy = ______________________________

Maximum Reward = ______________________________

Maximum Risk = ______________________________

Upside Breakeven = ______________________________

Downside Breakeven = ______________________________

Call Butterfly Spread: Long 1 Oct XYZ 45 Call @ 7, Short 2 Oct XYZ 55 Calls @ 5, Long 1 Oct XYZ 65 Call @ 1

Strategy = ______________________________

Maximum Reward = ______________________________

Maximum Risk = ______________________________

Upside Breakeven = ______________________________

Downside Breakeven = ______________________________

Put Butterfly Spread: Long 1 Sept XYZ 40 Put @ 1, Short 2 Sept XYZ 50 Puts @ 4, Long 1 Sept XYZ 60 Put @ 6

Strategy = ______________________________

Maximum Reward = ______________________________

Maximum Risk = ______________________________

Upside Breakeven = ______________________________

Downside Breakeven = ______________________________

Strategy Reviews

Bear Call Spread

Strategy = Buy a higher strike call and sell a lower strike call with the same expiration date.

Market Opportunity = Look for a bearish market where you anticipate a decrease in the price of the underlying asset below the strike price of the short call option.

Maximum Risk = Limited [(difference in strike prices × 100) – net credit].

Maximum Profit = Limited to the net credit received.

Breakeven = Lower call strike price + net credit received.

Margin = Required. Amount subject to broker's discretion.

Bull Put Spread

Strategy = Buy a lower strike put and sell a higher strike put with the same expiration date.

Market Opportunity = Look for a bullish market where you anticipate an increase in the price of the underlying asset above the strike price of the short put option.

Maximum Risk = Limited [(difference in strike prices × 100) – net credit].

Maximum Profit = Limited to the net credit received when the market closes above the short put option.

Breakeven = Higher put strike price – net credit received.

Margin = Required. Amount subject to broker's discretion.

Long Butterfly

Strategy = Buy a higher strike option at resistance, sell two lower strike options at equilibrium, and buy an even lower strike option at support (all calls or all puts).

Market Opportunity = Look for a range-bound market that is expected to stay between the breakeven points.

Maximum Risk = Limited to the net debit paid.

Maximum Profit = Limited [(difference in strikes × 100) – net debit paid]. Profit exists between breakevens.

Upside Breakeven = Highest strike price – net debit paid.

Downside Breakeven = Lowest strike price + net debit paid.

Margin = Required. Amount subject to broker's discretion.

Long Iron Butterfly

Strategy = Buy a higher strike call at resistance, sell an ATM strike call, sell a lower strike put, and buy an even lower strike put at support.

Market Opportunity = Look for a range-bound market that you anticipate to stay between the breakeven points.

Maximum Risk = Limited [(difference in strikes × 100) – net credit received]. Profit exists between breakevens.

Maximum Profit = Limited to the net credit received.

Upside Breakeven = Strike price of middle short call + net credit.

Downside Breakeven = Strike price of middle short put – net credit.

Margin = Required. Amount subject to broker's discretion.

Media Assignment

The media thrives on reporting sensational events. In the financial markets, the press tends to focus on periods when stock prices are falling and volatility is perceived to be high. Today, with roughly half of all Americans owning stocks in one form or another, the media has a receptive audience. After all, falling stock prices mean lost wealth, and stock market crashes cause a fair amount of uncertainty or anxiety among a great number of Americans. For that reason, when the market slides, the financial press tends to dramatize the situation and, in many cases, make it seem worse than it actually is.

The volatility trader does not get caught up in the media hype. Occasional falling stock prices are a fact of life in the market and are, therefore, inevitable. In fact, stocks fall roughly one-third of the time. Instead of becoming stricken with fear, the volatility trader understands that profit opportunities arise in the market whether prices are rising or falling and whether volatility is high or low. The key to achieving continuous success is to arm oneself with a variety of strategies that can profit in any market situation. In this chapter, the attention turns to high volatility strategies.

In order to develop a framework for trading high volatility, this media assignment encourages the reader to continue paper trading. Before developing paper trades, however, the first step is to define what a high volatility situation actually is. The measure, again, is implied volatility (IV), which is derived from the option prices in the market and the Black-Scholes or other options pricing model. There are two ways to identify stocks that have options with high IV. The first is to look through the headlines from the financial press—such as the Interactive Wall Street Journal, Bloomberg.com, or any other financial news source discussed in the early chapters of this workbook. Stocks that have recently exhibited large price moves are often the subject of commentary in the news media. Once those stocks are identified, a look at the IV of those options—by using an options calculator or Optionetics.com Platinum—can help determine whether implied volatility is high. Again, statistical volatility and past levels of IV are the two barometers used. The second way to find high volatility is the free ranker on the Optionetics.com home page. There, the reader can screen for stocks with high IV.

Once high volatility stocks are identified, it's time to paper trade the strategies discussed in this chapter. If implied volatility is high, the strategist wants to be a net seller of options. Therefore, the strategies include covered calls, naked puts, credit spreads, and butterflies. For example, if implied volatility is high and the option strategist has a bullish view on the stock, it is time to paper trade covered calls, bull put spreads, or naked puts (with the intention of either seeing the puts expire worthless or having the stock assigned). By contrast, if the strategist is bearish during a high volatility situation, the bear call spread is appropriate. Finally, after implied volatility has spiked higher and you expect it to consolidate and stay within a trading range, paper trade the iron butterfly. Again, the idea is to (1) keep adding to your arsenal of trading strategies and (2) learn which strategies best fit your personal investment style without putting your hard-earned money immediately at risk.

Vocabulary List

Please define the following terms:

- Bear call spread
- Bull put spread
- Call butterfly spread
- Covered call
- Credit spread
- Forward volatility skew
- Iron butterfly spread
- Margin
- Margin call
- Naked put
- Put butterfly spread
- Reverse volatility skew

10

Volatility Skews

Summary

Congratulations! If you've made it this far into the workbook, you have certainly covered a lot of ground. In fact, in terms of options trading knowledge, an understanding of the principles outlined in the first nine chapters of this workbook places you in the top 10% of all options traders. The reader has been introduced to a number of important tools and concepts including indicators that can help to chart historical volatility, implied volatility, stocks, options, sentiment analysis, and reversion to the mean, as well as specific strategies to use in different settings. All work together to give the reader the foundation for becoming a volatility trader.

Now our attention turns to a concept discussed briefly in the preceding chapter: volatility skews. Used mostly by professional traders to identify trading opportunities, volatility skews occur when two or more options on the same underlying stock or index have sizable differences in implied volatility. To identify skews, the strategist looks at various quotes across a series of options to find each option contract's implied volatility. When there is a big difference between one option and another, a skew exists. If so, trading opportunities arise that consist of purchasing the option with the lower volatility and simultaneously selling the option with the higher volatility.

There are two types of volatility skews to look for: volatility price skews and volatility time skews. Price skews exist when the implied volatility differs across strike prices of options on the same stock and the same expiration months. Time skews are identified by different levels of implied volatility on stock options with the same strike prices, but different expiration months. In this chapter, the reader learns how to identify each of these volatility skews, how to evaluate them, and of course, how to implement trading strategies using volatility skews.

Questions and Exercises

1. True or False: A volatility skew is created when two or more options on the same underlying stock or index have no difference in terms of implied volatility.

2. True or False: On the volatility smile skew graph, the higher the volatility, the steeper the skew is likely to be.

3. A volatility frown skew graph represents low IV options that are ___________ the at-the-money strike price.

   A. The same as

   B. Above

   C. Below

   D. Nowhere near

   E. Above and below

4. True or False: The volatility frown is the most common skew graph.

5. The volatility slope skew graph goes in ___________ direction(s).

   A. No apparent

   B. One

   C. Two

   D. A consistently upward

   E. A consistently downward

6. True or False: The best way to take advantage of skew is to remember the simple rule: Buy high (implied volatility) and sell low (implied volatility).

7. True or False: Volatility skews between months happen when the options with the same strike price but different expiration months have different levels of implied volatility.

8. A horizontal spread involves the purchase of a ___________ and the sale of a ___________ with the same strike price.

   A. Longer-term call/Shorter-term call

   B. Shorter-term call/Longer-term call

   C. Longer-term put/Shorter-term put

   D. Shorter-term call/Longer-term put

   E. None of the above

9. True or False: Diagonal spreads involve different strike prices.

10. Diagonal spreads using calls can be created if there is a volatility skew between the ____________ and the strategist is ____________ on the stock.
    - A. Short-term and long-term options/Bullish
    - B. Short-term and long-term options/Bearish
    - C. Higher and lower strike options/Bullish
    - D. Higher and lower strike options/Bearish
11. The primary objective of the calendar spread is to have time eat away at the ____________ option while the ____________ option retains its value.
    - A. Call/Put
    - B. Long/Short
    - C. Put/Call
    - D. Short/Long
    - E. None of the above
12. The maximum risk of a calendar spread is equal to ____________.
    - A. Difference in strikes minus net debit
    - B. Net debit divided by number of long-term options times 100
    - C. Stock price minus strike price
    - D. Long premium minus short premium
    - E. Long-term premium plus short-term premium
13. A calendar spread can lose money if ____________.
    - A. The stock price moves too low before the short call expires
    - B. The stock price doesn't move much before the short call expires
    - C. The stock price moves too high before the short call expires
14. True or False: The put calendar spread is appealing if expectations are that the stock will rise.
15. Name two keys to creating successful calendar spreads.
    1. ____
    2. ____
16. The types of volatility skews that can be useful in finding trading opportunities are ____________.
    - A. Volatility price skews
    - B. Volatility time skews
    - C. Volatility sell skews
    - D. A and B
    - E. A, B, and C

17. True or False: The strike prices for a set of options cannot have different levels of implied volatility.

18. When trading resumed following the terrorist attacks of September 11, 2001, volatility ____________.

    A. Dropped

    B. Remained the same

    C. Rose

    D. Was nonexistent

    E. None of the above

19. True or False: Demand will never cause a volatility skew.

20. Philip Morris is often considered a defensive stock because ____________.

    A. Smoking is a popular habit.

    B. It generally performs well when most stocks head lower.

    C. Tobacco companies are major contributors to political campaigns.

    D. The company is well known for its commitment to community service.

    E. More people smoke cigarettes when the stock market heads south.

Media Assignment

There is no substitute for actual trading to gain experience and expertise in options trading. Reading this workbook, solving the problems, and paper trading can give you the knowledge you need to trade successfully. However, the final piece of the puzzle is perhaps the most difficult. It involves putting your hard-earned money to work and sometimes experiencing losses. All traders have trades turn against them at some point or another. When paper trading, which has been the method encouraged throughout the media assignments in this book, bad trades are disappointing—but there are no direct financial consequences. Unfortunately, there is no way to teach real-world trading without actually experiencing it.

Therefore, in addition to paper trading the strategies discussed in the chapter, the next media assignment involves the somewhat merciless task of finding a brokerage firm for implementing your real-world trades. After reading this chapter, you should have added a number of new strategies to the repertoire. These include diagonal and calendar spreads. Each is used once a specific volatility skew is identified. With those strategies, and the ones discussed throughout the first nine chapters, the reader is armed with an arsenal of trades that can be used to generate profits in any market environment. Now, the goal is to find a broker who will execute those trades that best fit your trading style.

In today's marketplace, option traders can choose from full-service, discount, and online brokers. For the active options trader, the full-service or traditional Wall Street firms will charge relatively high commissions for option trades. Therefore, we generally recommend trading through an online broker. Not only are the commissions less, but many have charting, research, and other online tools that can be helpful when searching for potential trades. One comprehensive resource for screening potential online brokers is the book *Trade Options Online* by George Fontanills. In addition, Optionetics.com has a brokerage review section that provides details concerning the major players in online options brokerage. The act of searching for the best broker is sometimes an arduous and time-consuming task and will depend on your personal trading style and needs. Nevertheless, when searching, there are a number of telling questions to ask potential brokers.

- *Do your commissions vary depending on the number of trades placed each month or quarter?*
- *How fast are orders being executed?* Losing an eighth or a quarter of a point on every trade because your broker fails to act promptly can cost you a lot of money. A first-rate broker delivers exceptional executions.
- *Do you get paid for order flow?* Payment for order flow is a relationship between the brokerage firm and market makers. It has been criticized because it represents a conflict of interest for the brokerage firm. Specifically, rather than shopping the order around to competing market makers or ECNs in an effort to find the best possible price for the stock, the order is sent to a wholesale market maker. In exchange for the order, the market maker pays the broker for sending the orders. For example, say your brokerage firm has an arrangement with a large market maker and receives payments for orders. You submit an order to buy shares of Microsoft (MSFT) at the current market price. Your broker sends the order directly to the market maker without shopping around for the best possible price. In essence, even though it would be possible to get a slightly better price in a different market (ECN, market maker, etc.), the broker sends it directly to a preferred market maker and is compensated for routing the order their way. This is an important determinant because it can lead to conflicts of interest and poor execution of orders.
- *What are the terms of margin use?* The interest rates that brokers charge on margin accounts vary. The new account agreement spells out the terms. If it is unclear, ask.
- *Are you going to hit me with endless hidden fees?* Some brokers charge additional fees for things such as "postage and handling." What fees does the broker charge? Many will advertise ridiculously low commissions and then ding you right and left with fees.
- *What is the fee on an individual retirement account (IRA)?* Do you have an IRA that you would like to transfer to a broker? If so, what is the annual fee going to be on the IRA account? Some brokers offer no-fee IRAs. What kind of trades do they allow from an IRA? Some brokers allow options trading in IRAs, while others do not.

- *What do you mean by "real-time" quotes?* Some online brokers offer real-time market quotes. But some offer them only on the trades that you make. Other brokers offer real-time quotes only to accounts of a certain size. In short, quote services from brokerage firms vary. It can pay to look around to find the service that best suits your needs.

- *Do you provide research data or options data?* In addition to quotes, many brokerage firms provide other research and tools, but not all are equal in this respect. Are you better off paying the lowest commissions and getting your research elsewhere on the Web?

- *Do you accept stop or stop limit orders?* As a trader who trades online, do you understand the different types of orders you can place when buying and selling stock and options? Basically, stop and stop limit orders allow traders more flexibility. Stop, limit, stop-limit, good-till-canceled (GTC), or fill-or-kill (FOC) are all different ways to enter orders. Each gives the investor greater flexibility when entering and exiting trades. For example, a stop order provides the trader the ability to limit the losses associated with a position. If the trader is long shares of XYZ at $55 but does not want to hold the stock if it falls below $50, he or she can enter a stop loss order that specifically tells the broker to sell the stock if it falls below $50. That way, theoretically, it isn't necessary to watch each price change in the stock in order to limit potential losses.

- *Is the site user-friendly? Overall, is the site fast or slow?* If you are an active trader, chances are you will visit the broker site often. Dealing with a slow site can be detrimental to your trading profits.

- *Do you offer options-related tools or information?* Not many do, but some brokerage firms pride themselves in catering to options traders. Many that do assign a level of proficiency to each options trader. That is, you must be approved to trade options and option spreads. Find out what level you need to be to place the strategies reviewed in *The Volatility Course*.

- *Can your online service execute complex options orders? If so, what strategies?* Very few brokers offer the possibility of executing spreads, straddles, and combination strategies in one trade online. In these instances, speaking with a broker becomes necessary. Some brokers do have the capability, however, and if you are an active options trader, it may be worthwhile using one that provides complex ordering capabilities online.

Finding a reliable broker is sometimes the most challenging task new option traders face. Hopefully, the questions in this media assignment will help you overcome that challenge and find the one that is right for you. In addition, visit the online broker message boards at Optionetics.com. There you can find feedback from other options traders and objective commentary concerning the brokers that seem, at first glance, to fit your particular trading needs.

Vocabulary List

Please define the following terms:

- Back month
- Calendar spread
- Defensive stock
- Diagonal spread
- Front month
- Frown
- Horizontal spread
- Liquidity
- Options chain
- Slope
- Smile
- Volatility price skew
- Volatility time skew

Solutions and Discussions

1

Crisis and Chaos in Financial Markets

Answers and Discussions

1. The U.S. stock market suffered its greatest point decline in history on ____________.

   Answer: D—September 17, 2001

   Discussion: After the terrorist attacks of September 11, 2001, the stock market was closed for trading until September 17, 2001. During that time, there was a great deal of speculation on which way the market was likely to move—higher or lower. Many on Wall Street called for restraint on the part of investors. Indeed, some even urged investors not to sell stocks out of patriotism. Unfortunately, the devastation and economic uncertainty triggered by the terrorist assault was too much for most investors to stomach: They sold stock. When the markets reopened, the Dow Jones Industrial Average tumbled 684 points and suffered its worst point decline in history.

2. True or False: The bear market that preceded the Great Depression of the 1930s began on September 29, 1929, and lasted until June 1938.

   Answer: False

   Discussion: On October 29, 1929, during what became known as Black Tuesday, the stock market crashed. A three-year bear market that ended in June 1932 followed the crash. During that time, stocks fell, on average, 86%.

3. What is an index, and why are indexes helpful when it comes to studying the stock market?

Answer: Trying to make sense of which stocks are rising or falling on a daily basis is best accomplished by viewing stocks collectively. An index is a group of stocks that make up a portfolio in which performance can be monitored based on one calculation. The group can be designed to reflect the performance of the entire market, a specific sector, or an industry group.

Discussion: Indexes have been around since the late nineteenth century when Charles Dow created the Dow Jones Transportation Average and Industrial Average. Today, there are a large number of different indexes that investors can use to gauge the performance of the stock market. In addition, many indexes have options linked to their performances. Therefore, today indexes can be used in two ways:

1. As barometers for the performance of the market, sector, or industry groups.
2. As trading vehicles for index option strategies.

4. True or False: Rising interest rates hurt stock market investors.

   Answer: True

   Discussion: Rising interest rates have been the longtime nemesis of stock market investors. Higher rates hurt corporate profits by slowing down the economy and business activity. Weakening profits, in turn, often result in stock market declines. Rising interest rates also make alternative investments that pay fixed interest—such as certificates of deposit, bonds, and notes—more attractive relative to stocks.

5. The primary goal of the Federal Reserve is to ____________.

   Answer: D—All of the above (stabilize prices, promote economic growth, and strive for full employment)

   Discussion: The Federal Reserve is the nation's central bank. Its responsibilities are numerous. First, the Federal Reserve has a mandate to keep inflation in check. Rising inflation erodes the value of the dollar and is a danger to the U.S. economy. The primary tool for controlling inflation is monetary policy implemented through changes in interest rates (the federal funds rate). Most often, during periods of strong economic growth and rising inflation, the Federal Reserve will raise the fed funds rate to slow down the economy and quell the rising tide of inflation. But when the economy starts to sputter and business activity slows down, the Federal Reserve must also take action. Again, the primary tool for doing so is the federal funds rate (although the Fed can also add to the nation's money supply and change the discount rate). Theoretically, lower rates have a stimulating effect on the economy.

6. Prior to the market slide from September 2000 until September 2001, the market was vulnerable and eventually collapsed because of ____________.

   Answer: C—Rising interest rates

Discussion: Faced with a runaway stock market, a robust U.S. economy, and rising inflation, the Federal Reserve raised interest rates on six occasions from June 1999 to May 2000. The net result was a slowdown in the U.S. economy, business activity, and corporate profits. As it became clear that the robust earnings growth the stock market had experienced throughout the 1990s was about to reach an end, investors started to question the high prices afforded to the shares of some companies—especially within the technology sector. The net result was a stock market swoon that drove the Standard & Poor's 500 index down 36% between March 2000 and September 2001.

7. As a general rule, a bull market is identified by a ___________ rise from a low in the Dow Jones Industrial Average or other measure of the market.

   Answer: C—20%

   Discussion: This is a technical number and is computed as (high minus low)/low. A rise of 20% or more is enough to qualify as a bull market. Traders often talk of "bull" and "bear" markets when describing trends in the stock market. Bull markets are prolonged periods when stocks move higher. During bull markets, it makes sense to be a buyer of stocks because the momentum is pushing prices higher. The reason they are called "bull" markets is because the beast bucks up with its horns.

8. As a general rule, a bear market is identified by a ___________ decline from a high in the Dow Jones Industrial Average or other measure of the market.

   Answer: C—20%

   Discussion: This is a technical number and is computed as (high minus low)/high. A drop of 20% or more is enough to qualify as a bear market. Bear markets are long-term downward movements in the stock market. During bear markets, volatility is perceived to be high and investors are losing wealth. Momentum is driving prices lower, and it generally pays to be out of the market. Short selling along with bearish or neutral option strategies (discussed later in Chapter 8 and 9) work best during bear markets. The name stems from the fact that bears swat down with their claws.

9. Can volatility in one financial market spread to other markets, or does it remain isolated? Why?

   Answer: Volatility can spread because of contagion.

   Discussion: Due to technology and the growing interrelationship between global financial markets, there is a tendency for stock markets to move in concert. As a result, when an earnings warning from a prominent U.S.-based company such as Motorola rattles U.S. markets, sometimes shares of Asian and European chip makers and wireless companies follow the U.S. market lower. Indeed, in a global market, economic and profit news from one country has implications for the rest of the world.

10. True or False: Ultimately, the stock market falls more than it rises.

    Answer: False

    Discussion: Historically, the stock market has tended to rise more than it has fallen. In fact, the stock market rises two-thirds of the time and falls one-third of the time.

11. The world's largest auction-style stock exchange dates back to the Buttonwood Agreement of 1792. Today it is known as the ____________.

    Answer: A—New York Stock Exchange

    Discussion: The history of the New York Stock Exchange dates back to 1792 when five securities began being traded under a buttonwood tree near 68 Wall Street. This trading activity was first housed in a rented room at 40 Wall Street in 1817. The organization formally became the New York Stock Exchange in 1863.

12. True or False: Volatility equals risk.

    Answer: False

    Discussion: Volatility falls along a spectrum. There are periods of high volatility and periods of low volatility. The financial press is generally drawn to the episodes when the market swings wildly and volatility is high. Additionally, periods of high volatility are generally associated with falling stock prices and risk. However, volatility can also be high when stocks are moving sharply higher. Therefore, for the volatility trader, periods of high volatility do not necessarily mean risk for two reasons:

    1. There are option strategies that profit from high volatility.
    2. High volatility can also occur when stocks or the markets jump dramatically higher.

13. True or False: It is usually profitable to bet against the financial system over the long term.

    Answer: False

    Discussion: Despite market crashes and other periods of stock declines, the stock market has continually risen, and the system has survived intact. In fact, over the years the financial system has not only survived, but prospered as well. When developing investment strategies, this is an important concept to understand. That is, over the long run, it pays to be active in the system and implementing innovative option trading strategies, rather than living in fear with money sitting idle in a bank account or under a mattress.

14. Briefly describe why rising and falling markets are named "bull" and "bear."

    Answer: Bulls buck up with their horns. Bears swat down with their claws.

    Discussion: Bull and bear markets can last from several months to several years. In a bull market, the stock market makes a steady climb higher, and shareholders are rewarded with regular profits. During such times, it pays to trade on the long side more than the short side of the market. It is better to be a buyer than a seller. Often, in a bull market, profits are easy to generate and almost any investor—stock market, mutual fund, or options trader—is making money. Bear markets, however, are sometimes painful for most investors to endure. Stock prices fall week after week, and stock portfolios suffer losses. In this case, while the majority of investors feel the pain of lost wealth, the volatility trader can prosper by using option strategies that profit regardless of the direction of the market.

Media Assignment

Later, the reader will learn how to quantify and measure volatility. For now, the goal is to understand the factors that can cause it to rise and fall. The stock market is a discounting mechanism. As investors digest the arrival of new information, they make buying and selling decisions accordingly. As a result, unusual or unexpected information can cause investors to drastically alter their outlooks on the market, and aggressive buying or selling ensues.

For the trader, the important question to answer is, "What is moving the market now?" Sometimes market movements are appropriate. Other times the buying and selling are based on emotion and are, therefore, irrational. In the latter case, trading opportunities invariably arise. The key is to stay in tune with the day-to-day happenings in the market while keeping a long-term viewpoint. Doing so will help the trader to understand whether periods of high (or low) volatility are reasonable and sustainable or likely to be short-lived.

Vocabulary Definitions

Bear market: A sustained period of time in which stock prices move lower. A bear market is generally defined as a 20% decline from a previous high in the S&P 500, Dow Jones Industrial Average, or other broad measure of the U.S. stock market.

Black Tuesday: On October 29, 1929, in what in now known as Black Tuesday, the stock market crashed and paved the way for a three-year bear market that ended in June 1932.

Bloody Monday: Monday, October 19, 1987, when, on one day, the Dow Jones Industrial Average plunged from 2,247 to 1,739, or 22.6%.

Bull market: A period lasting from several months to several years in which the stock market moves higher. Technical analysts consider a move of 20% from a previous low to qualify as a bull market.

Buy and hold: A traditional investment discipline that calls for buying stocks at attractive prices and holding them for a period of years or decades. Buy and hold advocates attempt to profit from the fact that stock prices have historically moved higher.

Chicago Board Options Exchange (CBOE): Established in 1973, the Chicago Board Options Exchange is the world's first and largest options exchange (www.cboe.com).

Commodities: Grains, metals, minerals, and other unprocessed, unfinished goods that are generally used as raw materials. Commodities trade in financial markets in large amounts.

Contagion: A term popularized during the Global Financial Crisis of 1998 when stock markets in one part of the world triggered declines in other parts of the world. Like a cold that passes from one student to the next in a classroom, technology and globalization have created a growing linkage between financial markets worldwide.

Correction: A move lower in a bull market ranging between 5% and 20% or an advance in a bear market between 5% and 20%.

Dow Jones Industrial Average: A price-weighted average of 30 of the largest stocks trading on the New York Stock Exchange and Nasdaq Stock Market. First developed in 1896, it is one of the most widely watched barometers for the performance of the U.S. stock market. Also known as the Dow or the Industrial Average.

Exchange-traded funds (ETF): A pooled investment vehicle that represents ownership of a portfolio of stocks. Investors buy and sell shares of ETFs through brokers. Additionally, shares of exchange-traded funds trade on the organized stock exchanges and are bought and sold like stocks.

Federal Reserve: The central bank of the United States that controls the nation's monetary policy and credit through bank reserves, money supply, and interest rates. But just what is the Federal Reserve? Most people believe that it is the branch of the U.S. government charged with making monetary policy decisions. Most people are wrong. While it's true that the Federal Reserve makes monetary policy, it is an independent group. The U.S. government was on the verge of bankruptcy back in the early 1900s when 12 very wealthy families stepped forward to bail out the government. The Federal Reserve, officially created by Congress in 1913, consists of 12 district banks as well as a Board of Governors. Alan Greenspan is the current Fed chairman. The primary goals of the Federal Reserve are to stabilize prices, promote economic growth, and strive for full employment. These goals are accomplished through managing monetary policy, which is implemented by the Federal Open Market Committee (FOMC). The FOMC consists of 12 members: seven members of the Fed's Board of Governors, the president of the Federal Reserve Bank of New York, and four presidents out of the 11 other district banks. These four presidents each serve a one-year term on a rotating basis.

The Federal Reserve (the Fed) attempts to achieve a balance between low inflation and economic growth. One tool for doing so is open market operations. Open market operations means the buying or selling of government securities to control liquidity in the economy. That's what is happening when you hear that liquidity (or money supply) is going up or down in the economy. When liquidity is high, it makes it easier for businesses to borrow money, which in turn leads to more R&D spending, which leads to growth. Another tool of the Federal Reserve is the fed funds rate. You often hear the terms "easing" and "tightening" in reference to Fed policy. These terms refer to changes in the fed funds rate and not the open market operations. The fed funds rate is the rate of interest on overnight loans on excess reserves. Excess reserves refers to the amount of money held in banks that exceeds the set requirements by the Fed. Since the Federal Reserve has considerable control over the availability of federal funds, this rate is considered an important indicator of Federal Reserve policy and the direction of future interest rates. When the Fed is easing, it is lowering the fed funds rate and making it easier to borrow money. When it is tightening, the Fed is raising interest rates and making capital less available. In addition, while not the same as open market operations, easing does add liquidity to the system by lowering interest rates and making it easier for corporations and individuals to access capital (borrow money). Tightening has the opposite effect. Therefore, market watchers are continuously watching Fed policy (open market operations and the fed funds rate) to see if liquidity is being added to, or taken away from, the financial markets.

Fed funds rate: Largely controlled by the Federal Reserve, it is the rate on overnight loans on excess reserves held by commercial banks in the United States. The rate is considered another primary tool for the monetary policy of the Federal Reserve. When it falls, it suggests that the Federal Reserve is trying to stimulate the U.S. economy. Conversely, when the Federal Reserve is increasing the federal funds rate it is attempting to cool the economy and/or tame inflation.

Futures markets: The buying and selling of futures contracts, each of which is an agreement to take delivery of a commodity on a future date. There are a number of organized futures exchanges in the United States. For example, the Chicago Board of Trade lists trading on grains such as oats, corn, and wheat. Other futures exchanges are the Chicago Mercantile Exchange, the New York Mercantile Exchange, and the Kansas City Board of Trade.

Global financial crisis: An episode in the fall of 1998 in which stock markets around the globe fell in tandem. Currency troubles in one part of the world triggered similar problems in other nations. Stock markets fell, and the carnage eventually hit U.S. shores.

Index fund: A mutual fund designed to mirror the performance of an index such as the Dow Jones Industrial Average or the S&P 500.

Liquidity: (1) The amount of cash within an account, economy, or portfolio. The more cash, the greater the liquidity. (2) The ability to quickly convert an investment to cash. Stocks and options are generally considered liquid investments because they can easily be converted to cash. (3) The amount of trading associated with a given investment security. The greater the trading volume of a stock or option, the greater its liquidity.

Long Term Capital Management: A well-known hedge fund that folded during the global financial crisis of 1998 due to mistimed bets in credit markets around the world. The managers of the fund were considered to be among the brightest and most sophisticated in the financial world—the rocket scientists of Wall Street. The Federal Reserve and major investment banks eventually bailed out the fund to avoid a global financial catastrophe.

Margin: The amount of money deposited to purchase investment securities or the amount of equity held in a brokerage account. Margin is used to determine the amount of securities that investors can purchase on credit.

Margin call: The request for additional funds in a margined account. Margin calls occur when the equity value in an account has dropped below a minimum requirement or when additional securities are purchased on credit.

Mutual fund: A pooled investment vehicle that consists of a portfolio of stocks, bonds, cash, or a combination of the three. A portfolio or fund manager makes the investment decisions. Investors buy and sell mutual fund shares through a broker or a mutual fund company. Open-end mutual funds are purchased through a broker or the mutual fund company and *do not* trade on the exchanges. Closed-end funds are purchased through a broker and *do* trade on the stock exchanges. The name "open-end" comes from the fact that, since a mutual fund company is in charge of selling shares, it is continually open to new investors. As more money flows into the fund, new shares are issued. This is not true of closed-end funds, which have a fixed number of shares trading in the stock market. Open-end funds far outnumber closed-end funds.

Nifty Fifty: Glamorized during the bull market of the early 1970s, the Nifty Fifty were 50 of the largest growth stocks trading on the U.S. exchanges. They were considered to be among the favorite holdings of large investors such as mutual funds and pension funds. The Nifty Fifty included companies such as General Electric, Exxon Mobil, and Intel. It is not currently used to describe large cap stocks trading today.

Options: Options are derivatives that will change in value based on changes in the value of an underlying asset (stock, index, or future) and fluctuations in volatility. They also represent a contract between two parties to buy or sell an asset (stock, index, or future) at a predetermined price for a specific period of time. Options are traded on exchanges and can be purchased or sold through a stock brokerage firm. The price of an option will change daily due to a number of factors, but the price of an option is mostly a function of the price of the underlying asset. Additionally, there are two types of options: puts and calls. A call option gives the owner the right, but not the obligation, to *buy* a stock, index, or future at a specific price (known as the strike price) until the expiration of that option. The contract must be fulfilled before the expiration date, which is generally by close of business prior to the third Saturday of the option's expiration month. For example, a call option that expires in January 2003 ceases to exist after January 17, 2003—or the third Friday of the expiration month. A put option, by contrast, gives the owner the right, but not the obligation, to *sell* the underlying asset at a specific price for a predetermined period of time or before the option expires. The maximum risk of buying an option is limited to the price paid to buy the option: the premium. Conversely, sellers of puts and calls have an obligation to fulfill the terms of the contract. For example, a seller of calls must be prepared to sell (deliver) the underlying asset at a specific price (strike price) until the option expires. Similarly, the put seller must honor the terms of the options contract—buy (accept delivery of) the stock at a predetermined price prior to expiration. When an option seller is required to fulfill the terms of the contract, it is known as assignment. However, since options trade on exchanges, they can be closed at any time prior to being assigned. For example, the call seller can buy his or her calls at any time prior to expiration. Doing so will end the seller's commitment to the contract.

Prime rate: The rate commercial banks charge customers with the highest credit quality. Generally considered a benchmark for other rates, including mortgage rates.

Pullback: A move lower in a bull market of 5% or less or an advance in a bear market of 5% or less.

S&P 500: A market-value weighted average of 500 of the largest stocks trading on the U.S. stock exchanges. Developed by Standard & Poor's, the index is used as a gauge for the performance of the stock market and a benchmark for the relative performance of professional investors such as mutual funds, portfolio managers, and pension funds.

2

Volatility in the Stock Market

Answers and Discussions

1. Name the three indexes (and their ticker symbols) reporters most often use to comment on the performance of the stock market.

   Answers:

   1. Dow Jones Industrial Average ($INDU)
   2. Nasdaq Composite ($COMPQ)
   3. Standard & Poor's 500 ($SPX)

   Discussion: The Dow, Nasdaq, and S&P 500 are the three most common barometers for the stock market. Indeed, these three indexes are the ones most often cited in the financial press and on the evening news. Additionally, quotes for each can be found throughout the day by typing their ticker symbols into a quote box on a number of financial-related sites, including Optionetics.com, Yahoo! Finance (http://finance.yahoo), and the Chicago Board Options Exchange (www.cboe.com).

2. By recent estimates ____________ of all American households own stocks in one form or another today.

   Answer: C—50%

   Discussion: Prior to the 1930s, stocks were considered speculative. Investors bought bonds; others just held cash. Today, however, that has changed. Nearly one-half of all Americans own stocks in one form or another—through either retirement plans, mutual funds, or shares.

3. When a company wants to start selling shares of stock to the public, it issues the ____________.

   Answer: A—Initial public offering (IPO)

   Discussion: In order to raise capital, companies often turn to financial markets. Sometimes the process involves the issuance of bonds, or debt obligations. Other times, a firm decides to sell off part of the company to the public by issuing shares. It hires an investment bank and sells shares to the public through an initial public offering (IPO). After the offering, shares are listed on one of the stock exchanges—the Nasdaq Stock Market, New York Stock Exchange, or American Stock Exchange—and are made available for trading.

4. Name the three principal stock exchanges.

   Answers:

   1. New York Stock Exchange (NYSE)
   2. American Stock Exchange (AMEX)
   3. Nasdaq Stock Market

   Discussion: Of the three principal stock exchanges in the United States, two are auction-style markets where trading takes place on an exchange floor—the NYSE and AMEX. One is an electronic exchange consisting of a network of market makers—the Nasdaq Stock Market.

5. As an off-floor trader, you buy at the ____________ price and sell at the ____________ price.

   Answer: A—Ask/Bid

   Discussion: Market makers have positions in the trading pits on the exchange floors (the Chicago Board Options Exchange, the Philadelphia Stock Exchange, or the American Stock Exchange). An off-floor trader is someone who does not have a professional position working on the exchange floor. Stock and options traders are always fighting the spread. The spread is the difference between the bid and the asking price. The bid is the price the market maker or specialist is willing to buy the stock or option for. That is what market makers are bidding. The ask, on the other hand, is what it costs the trader or investor to buy the stock or option. It is what is being asked. Bids and asks for any stock or option are available through almost any quote service.

6. Match the terms with their respective definitions in Table 2.3.

Table 2.3 Match Term to Definition—Answer

Data	*Definition*
Last	E. The last price that the security traded for at the exchange.
Open	H. The price of the first transaction of the current trading day.
Change	N. The amount the last sale differs from the previous trading day's closing price.
% Change	C. The percentage the price has changed since the previous day's closing price.
High	B. The highest price for the current trading day.
Low	M. The lowest price for the current trading day.
Bid	A. The highest price a prospective buyer (floor trader) is prepared to pay for a specified time for a trading unit of a specified security.
Ask	F. The lowest price acceptable to a prospective seller (floor trader) of a security.
52-Week High	O. The highest price the stock traded at in the past 52-week period.
52-Week Low	K. The lowest price the stock traded at in the past 52-week period.
Earnings per Share	D. The bottom line (net pretax profit) divided by the number of shares outstanding.
Volume	I. The total number of shares traded in a day.
Shares Outstanding	G. The total number of shares the company has issued.
Market Cap	P. Shares outstanding multiplied by the closing stock price.
P/E Ratio	L. Stock price divided by the earnings per share.
Exchange	J. This indicates where a company lists, or registers, its shares.

7. The purpose of computing an index is to measure the performance of ____________.

   Answer: D—All of the above (an entire group of stocks, a specific sector of stocks, and a specific industrial sector of stocks)

   Discussion: Since Charles Dow created the first index in 1884—the Dow Jones Transportation Average—brokerage firms and financial services companies have created a large number of other indexes. Some are designed to gauge the performance of the entire market; examples include the S&P 500, the Dow Jones Industrial Average, and the Wilshire 5000. Others have been created to measure narrower groups of stocks, such as stocks within specific industry groups. Examples of sector indexes include the PHLX Semiconductor index, the AMEX Biotechnology index, and the CBOE Internet index.

8. True or False: The Russell 2000 is an index that primarily tracks the performance of small cap stocks.

   Answer: True

   Discussion: Developed by the Frank Russell Company of Tacoma, Washington, the "Russell" is an index consisting of 2,000 stocks—the 3,000 largest companies trading on the U.S. exchanges with the top 1,000 removed. It is considered a barometer for the performance of smaller companies.

9. True or False: An index can be used as an investment.

   Answer: False

   Discussion: Unlike stocks, indexes cannot be bought and sold. They represent the aggregate performance of a group of stocks. Initially, indexes were computed as the simple average of stock prices. Today, however, the computation is more sophisticated and requires the use of a divisor—which helps account for stock splits, dividends, and mergers. Although an index is not an investment vehicle, in certain situations investors can participate in the rise or fall in an index through index funds, exchange-traded funds, or index options.

10. Match the indexes with their respective ticker symbols in Table 2.4.

Table 2.4 Match Index to Symbol—Answer

Index Name	*Symbol*
Dow Jones Industrial Average	$INDU
S&P 500	$SPX
Wilshire 5000	$TMW
New York Stock Exchange Composite	$NYA
Nasdaq Composite	$COMPQ
S&P 100	$OEX
Russell 3000	$RUA

11. ETF stands for ____________.

    Answer: D—Exchange-traded funds

    Discussion: Exchange-traded funds (ETFs) are pooled investment vehicles that represent ownership in a group of stocks. Investors buy and sell shares of ETFs. In addition, shares of exchange-traded funds trade on the organized stock exchanges and are bought and sold like stocks.

12. Investors seeking to own a basket of stocks that consists of mostly technology stocks can buy shares of ____________.

    Answer: C—QQQ

    Discussion: The Nasdaq 100 QQQ is one of the most popular investment vehicles as of this writing. Also known as the Qs, it is an exchange-traded fund that includes some of the most actively traded technology stocks. Specifically, QQQ consists of the Nasdaq 100, which is the 100 largest nonfinancial stocks trading on the Nasdaq Stock Market; 75% of those companies, in turn, are technology stocks, including Intel, Cisco Systems, and Microsoft.

13. What is the difference between HOLDRs and ETFs?

    Answer: Unlike ETFs, HOLDRs do not mirror the performance of a specific index.

Discussion: Brokerage firm Merrill Lynch developed Holding Company Depository Receipts (HOLDRs). They are ETFs because they represent an ownership in a portfolio of stocks, and their shares trade on the exchanges like stocks (but only in 100-share lots). HOLDRs are created around specific industry groups. For example, there are Broadband HOLDRs, Biotechnology HOLDRs, and Internet HOLDRs.

14. The most important factor in determining an asset's volatility is ____________.

    Answer: B—Price changes

    Discussion: Changes in the price of an asset determine its level of volatility. If the asset shows little price movement from one day to the next, it has low volatility—wide price swings equal high volatility.

15. The ____________ is the most common price used for computing volatility.

    Answer: B—Closing price

    Discussion: There are a number of ways for computing the volatility of an asset. Most measures consider only the closing price of the day. Therefore, if the stock opens at $50 a share, tumbles to $40 a share, and bounces back up to close for $50 a share, the intraday drop (from $50 to $40) will not enter the computation. Obviously, measuring volatility in this manner can be a drawback to the volatility trader because it does not capture the asset's true volatility. Nevertheless, the closing price is the most often used and most readily available price for computing most measures of volatility.

16. When there are long bars between high and low prices on a stock chart, volatility is____________.

    Answer: A—High

    Discussion: Bars on stock charts record the high and low prices of the trading day. When the bars are long, there is a wide difference between the high price (top of the bar) and the low price (bottom of the bar). A significant difference between the high and low price of a stock suggests relatively high volatility.

17. When important and relevant new information arrives to the market, volatility tends to ____________.

    Answer: A—Rise

    Discussion: New information is quickly incorporated into stock prices. When the information is unexpected, it will have the greatest impact on prices. For example, earnings surprises often cause a stock to jump dramatically higher or lower. The impact of a news event will vary based on its relative importance or significance and the degree to which it surprises investors.

18. True or False: Human emotion has no effect on volatility.

    Answer: False

Discussion: Fear and greed are two of the primary factors causing stock prices to change, and hence have an important effect on volatility.

19. Name and describe two ways of measuring volatility.

Answers:

1. Historical volatility gauges price movement in terms of past performance.
2. Implied volatility approximates how much the marketplace thinks prices will move.

Discussion: Statistical volatility is computed as the annualized standard deviation of past prices over a period of time (10, 30, or 90 days). It is considered a measure of historical volatility, because it looks at past prices. Discussed in terms of percentages, statistical volatility can be computed over different time frames; the number of days under consideration will vary depending on the trader's trading time frame. Implied volatility, on the other hand, is derived using an option's price, the strike price, and the time to expiration, along with the price of the underlying asset (accounting for dividends) and the prevailing interest rate (T-bill). Those variables are then plugged into an option pricing model (such as Black-Scholes) to arrive at a level of volatility implied by the option. Options on each individual stock or index will have a unique level of implied volatility.

20. The most common reason for a stock to fall precipitously is due to concern over ____________.

Answer: B—Earnings

Discussion: Like the elementary student bringing home periodic report cards, corporations deliver earnings results each quarter. When those earnings results disappoint investors, the result can sometimes trigger a violent move lower in the company's stock price. Indeed, profits are the primary driver underlying a stock's price. Investors are much more willing to own shares of companies that deliver steady earnings gains from one year to the next. Therefore, poor earnings generally lead to shareholder dismay and greater volatility in the company's stock price.

Media Assignment

At this point the investor should have access to quotes for stocks, indexes, and options. Importantly, to access quotes, the trader must also know ticker symbols. For stocks and indexes, this information is relatively easy to obtain using symbol lookup capabilities available on many Internet sites (including www.cboe.com, www.esignal.com, and www.optionetics.com). Symbols for options are a bit trickier and require three pieces of information—the root symbol, the strike price, and the expiration date.

The first part of an option symbol is known as the root symbol and represents the underlying stock. It is often similar to the actual ticker of the stock. For instance, the root symbol for International Business Machines is straightforward. It is the same as the stock symbol: IBM. Stocks with a four-letter ticker, however, always have root symbols different from their stock symbols because option root symbols can have one, two, or three letters, but never four. For instance, while the stock ticker symbol for Microsoft is MSFT, the option symbol is MSQ. The second part of an option symbol represents the month and defines whether the option is a put or a call. For example, a January call uses the letter A after the root symbol. Table 2.5 shows how each month (call or put) is assigned a different letter.

The final part of an option symbol represents the option's strike price. The number 5 is assigned the letter A, 10 the letter B, 15 the letter C, and so on. Therefore, the IBM January 95 call will have the symbol IBMAS. Table 2.6 provides the letters assigned to each strike price.

Understanding option symbols is but a first step in developing an understanding of the options market. One of the most important tools is the options chain. Many online brokerage firms and the aforementioned web sites offer the possibility to view the entire series of option contracts for any given stock symbol. For instance, an options chain on IBM will list all of the options for International Business Machines, separated into groups of puts and calls and sorted by expiration month and strike prices. This is known as an options chain. It is simply a matter of entering the stock symbol, viewing the chain, and understanding each option symbol. Doing so will allow the trader to compare prices across expiration dates and strike prices and help find the most suitable option contract for any specific strategy.

In addition, the option strategist wants to consider how prices change over time. Watching prices change on a day-to-day basis can help the trader understand how different events and the passage of time affect options' premiums. Remember that option prices are not stagnant; they change over time. That's why it is vital to have access to up-to-the-minute information from sites like www.cboe.com,

Table 2.5 Option Symbols—Months for Calls/Puts

	Jan.	*Feb.*	*Mar.*	*Apr.*	*May*	*Jun.*	*Jul.*	*Aug.*	*Sep.*	*Oct.*	*Nov.*	*Dec.*
Calls	A	B	C	D	E	F	G	H	I	J	K	L
Puts	M	N	O	P	Q	R	S	T	U	V	W	X

Table 2.6 Option Symbols II—Strike Prices

A	*B*	*C*	*D*	*E*	*F*	*G*	*H*	*I*	*J*	*K*	*L*	*M*
5	10	15	20	25	30	35	40	45	50	55	60	65
105	110	115	120	125	130	135	140	145	150	155	160	165
N	*O*	*P*	*Q*	*R*	*S*	*T*	*U*	*V*	*W*	*X*	*Y*	*Z*
70	75	80	85	90	95	100	$7\frac{1}{2}$	$12\frac{1}{2}$	$17\frac{1}{2}$	$22\frac{1}{2}$	$27\frac{1}{2}$	$32\frac{1}{2}$
170	175	180	185	190	195	200	$17\frac{1}{2}$	$112\frac{1}{2}$	$117\frac{1}{2}$	$122\frac{1}{2}$	$127\frac{1}{2}$	$132\frac{1}{2}$

www.optionetics.com, or www.esignal.com. Timely information is essential to making informed decisions.

After learning how to obtain stock and options quotes, the next step is to start the trading process by using online tools to scan the markets, create charts, and explore useful indicators.

Vocabulary Definitions

Ask: The price currently asked by a trader to sell a stock or option. Also known as the offer.

Bid: The current price a market maker is willing to accept as payment for a stock or option.

Closing price: The final or last price of the trading session for a stock, index, or option. Sometimes called the close.

Comovement: The tendency for two investment vehicles to exhibit similar price movements. For example, two semiconductor companies might have stocks with a high degree of comovement. Also known as covariance.

Derivative instruments: Investment vehicles that have values derived from other assets. For example, stock options are derivatives because their value is dependent on the value of another asset—stocks.

Historical volatility: Historical volatility is a measurement of how much a stock's price has fluctuated over a period of time in the past. There are different ways of measuring historical volatility, and all are designed to look at the volatility of an investment that has existed in the past. The most common measure for options traders is statistical volatility, which is computed as the annualized standard deviation of past prices over a period of time (10, 30, or 90 days), discussed in term of percentages. Statistical volatility can be computed over different time frames, and the number of days under consideration will vary depending on the option trader's trading time frame.

HOLDRs: Holding Company Depository Receipts (HOLDRs) are a type of exchange-traded fund (ETF). Shares can be bought and sold in round lots of 100 shares. Like a stock, HOLDRs are traded on the stock exchanges and are priced throughout the trading day. Investors can place orders to buy and sell shares in the same way they place stock orders. At the same time, however, with HOLDRs investors benefit from diversification, or spreading their risk across a number of stocks. HOLDRs are available on a number of different industry groups:

Biotechnology HOLDRs	BBH
Broadband HOLDRs	BDH
B2B Internet HOLDRs	BHH
Internet Architecture HOLDRs	IAH
Internet HOLDRs	HHH
Internet Infrastructure HOLDRs	IIH
Market 2000+ HOLDRs	MKH

Pharmaceutical HOLDRs	PPH
Regional Bank HOLDRs	RKH
Retail HOLDRs	RTH
Semiconductor HOLDRs	SMH
Software HOLDRs	SWH
Telecom HOLDRs	TTH
Utilities HOLDRs	UTH
Wireless HOLDRs	WMH

Implied volatility (IV): Implied volatility reflects not past volatility of an asset, but rather market expectations concerning what the asset's volatility is likely to be going forward. IV is computed using an option pricing model, such as Black-Scholes, and requires the following inputs: the option's price, the strike price of the option, and the time to expiration, along with the price of the underlying asset (accounting for dividends), and the prevailing interest rate (T-bill).

Index: Also known as an average or market average, an index is simply an average of a group of stock prices. There are three ways to construct an index: price-weighted, market-value weighted, and equal-dollar weighted methods. Each is unique, but all three are used to gauge the collective performance of a group of investment securities. An example is the PHLX Semiconductor index, which consists of 16 semiconductor stocks.

Initial public offering (IPO): The process through which a private company becomes a public company in an effort to raise capital to expand business operations. The IPO is a company's first sale of stock to the investment public. Smaller, young start-up companies often hire investment banks to complete an IPO.

Listing requirements: The requirements imposed by a stock exchange that a public company must adhere to in order to have its shares listed on the exchange. The requirements for each exchange vary and are generally related to the company's size (market value) and sales. When a publicly traded company falls below the exchange's listing requirements, it runs the risk of being delisted—having its stock removed from trading on the exchange.

Moving average: An average of a set of variables such as stock prices over time. The term "moving" stems from the fact that as each new price is added the first (or oldest) is deleted. For example, a 14-day average of closing prices is calculated by adding the last 14 closes and dividing that number by 14. The result is noted on a chart. The next day the same calculations are performed with the new result being connected (using a solid or dotted line) to yesterday's, and so forth. Technical analysts use moving averages to view the long-term performance of a stock or an index.

Open: The first price of the trading day for a stock, index, or option.

Private company: A company that has not gone public and therefore does not have shares listed on any of the exchanges.

Public company: A company that has issued shares to the public in order to raise capital.

Securities and Exchange Commission (SEC): The regulatory body in charge of overseeing the activity in the U.S. securities markets. It is a federal agency that administers securities laws in the United States. Created in 1934 under the Securities and Exchange Act, it is headed by five appointed members.

Spread: The difference between the bid and ask. It is sometimes possible to have orders executed within the spread. Market makers live on the spread.

Stock: An investment vehicle representing ownership interest in a publicly traded company.

Stock symbol: A one-, two-, three-, four-, or sometimes five-letter designation assigned to shares of publicly traded companies. Stock symbols are used to retrieve price quotes and to place buy and sell orders.

3

Historical Volatility

Answers and Discussions

1. True or False: When prices are rising and the majority of investors are making money, emotion (optimism and greed) drives prices lower.

   Answer: False

   Discussion: Theoretically, a stock's price is equal to its fundamentals. The fundamentals, in turn, relate to the company's earnings, dividends, assets, and other measures of financial strength. Ultimately, investors are continually assessing the stock's fundamentals and making buying and selling decisions, which make the stock price move higher or lower. The stock price, then, is continually changing as investors assess and reassess the company's prospects. However, at times the stock price will depart from the fundamentals. There are periods when the movement in the stock price, not the fundamentals, elicits a reaction from investors. During times when the stock price falls, shareholders are losing money. Sometimes a sharp drop in a stock can lead to panic and fear-based selling. Alternatively, when a stock or market is moving rapidly higher and investors are making money, there is a tendency for greed to take over and drive prices higher still. When the prices move too far beyond the fundamentals, there is a risk that the stock will correct and move lower.

2. True or False: When prices are falling, emotion (fear and panic) drives prices higher.

   Answer: False

   Discussion: Investors are attracted to activity. A stock that is moving sideways gets little attention from investors. A sharp rise in a stock, however, often attracts buyers; when a decline is rapid or violent, investors will often react out of fear and drive the price lower. Fear and greed are the two emotions that can drive stock prices lower or higher well beyond their fundamentals.

3. Historical volatility is also referred to as ___________.

   Answer: B—Actual volatility

   Discussion: Historical volatility is a measure of past prices and is sometimes referred to as the asset's actual volatility. Statistical volatility is a type of historical volatility, but not the only one. Average True Range, Bollinger bands, and beta are also discussed in the *The Volatility Course*. Although their names do not suggest volatility, they do measure the past volatility of a stock or index.

4. True or False: Historical volatility is computed using current stock prices.

   Answer: False

   Discussion: Historical volatility is derived from past, not current, prices.

5. Historical volatility measures a stock's propensity for ___________.

   Answer: D—Price movement

   Discussion: Historical volatility provides information regarding a stock's past price movement. When it is high, it says that the stock has been showing extreme fluctuations in price. When it is low, it suggests quiet or sideways trading. There are a number of ways to measure historical volatility, including Average True Range, Bollinger bands, and statistical volatility.

6. Implied volatility is priced into an option's value in the ___________.

   Answer: B—Present

   Discussion: Implied volatility is computed using an option pricing model such as Black-Scholes. In order to do so, the model requires the following inputs: the option's price, the strike price of the option, and the time to expiration, along with the price of the underlying asset (accounting for dividends), and the prevailing interest rate (T-bill). It is taken directly from the market prices in the options market and therefore reflects the level of volatility priced into present option prices.

7. When studying statistical volatility, it is important to consider it in light of ___________.

   Answer: D—All of the above (other stocks or indexes, past levels of historical volatility associated with that stock or index, and historical volatility within different time frames)

   Discussion: Each stock or index will have a unique level of volatility that changes over time. Comparing it to the statistical volatility of other stocks and indexes can tell you whether the stock or index is relatively volatile. Furthermore, viewing the statistical volatility of a stock over time will tell you whether the volatility of a stock is rising or falling. Similarly, looking at a stock's statistical volatility over different time periods will also provide information regarding trends in volatility. For instance, if the 10-day statistical volatility of a stock is 20% and the 100-day is 40%, the stock has recently witnessed a sharp decline in volatility.

8. True or False: Average True Range is exactly the same as statistical volatility.

   Answer: False

   Discussion: Average True Range considers open, high, and low prices of a stock or an index. Unlike statistical volatility, which considers only closing prices, ATR encompasses more information. In addition, Average True Range is generally plotted below the price chart of a stock or index. Statistical volatility is generally considered numerically and rarely shown on stock charts.

9. Moving averages are used to analyze ____________ over a specified period of time on an average basis.

   Answer: B—Price action

   Discussion: A moving average is a set of variables such as stock prices viewed over time. It is called a moving average because as each new price is added, the first (or oldest) is deleted. Technical analysts use moving averages of stock prices to study the long-term performance of a stock or an index.

10. Bollinger bands are moving ____________.

    Answer: C—Standard deviations

    Discussion: Bollinger bands are computed as the standard deviations of the moving averages. Standard deviation is a statistical term that means the variability of the distribution. Whether the stock has a high or low standard deviation, its price will remain within two standard deviations of its moving average 95% of the time according to statistical probabilities. Each day, as the moving average is updated, so are Bollinger bands.

11. When analyzing Bollinger bands, the trading strategist expects the bands will come together when the movement in the stock is ____________.

    Answer: B—Less volatile

    Discussion: Bollinger bands consist of two bands. One sits two standard deviations above the moving average and the other two standard deviations below the moving average. When the stock is showing less volatility, or less variability in price, the bands will narrow and suggest that the stock is beginning to trade within a narrower range.

12. When the movement of a stock becomes more volatile, Bollinger bands will become ____________.

    Answer: B—Wider

    Discussion: When the volatility of a stock rises, its price will fluctuate in a wider range. There will be a greater variability in its distribution, which will cause Bollinger bands to become wider.

13. True or False: A high beta stock is a high volatility stock and subject to greater percentage moves than the overall market.

    Answer: True

    Discussion: Beta is the measure of a stock's volatility relative to the overall market. For example, XYZ stock is two times more volatile than the market and has a beta of 2.00. Theoretically, when the market rises 5%, the XYZ will rise 10%. When the market declines 5%, XYZ will fall 10%. Therefore, a stock with a beta of more than 1.00 will experience greater percentage moves than the overall market.

Media Assignment

Charts are windows for viewing changes in a stock price or an index price. They can provide quick information concerning past price movement and volatility. In addition, using charting software, applying more complex indicators such as Bollinger bands and ATR is generally possible with the click of a mouse. Charts are essential to the volatility trader. Therefore, the aim of the latest media assignment is to find a reliable source of stock charts. In the end, the reader should be able to answer the following questions in the affirmative:

- Do you have access to stock charts?
- Can you create daily stock charts for IBM, Exxon Mobil, and General Electric?
- Can you create weekly and monthly charts for the Dow Jones Industrial Average?
- Have you plotted Bollinger bands, ATR, and moving averages for a basket of stocks and indexes?
- Does looking at a chart give you a good sense of whether the volatility of a stock is rising or falling?

Vocabulary Definitions

Average True Range (ATR): Developed by J. Welles Wilder Jr., Average True Range is used to gauge an asset's daily price swings. Although Wilder developed the ATR for commodities, the indicator is also used for stocks and indexes. A stock experiencing a high level of volatility will have a higher ATR, while a low volatility stock will have a low ATR. Most measures of historical volatility, such as statistical volatility, consider only the closing prices for a stock or index and fail to capture the volatility caused by sharp gaps (or days when the stock opens much higher or lower than the previous day's close). ATR, in contrast, considers the close, high, and low prices of the day. It is computed as the average of the True Range (TR) over a fixed number of days. TR is computed as the greatest of: (1) the distance from the current day's high to the current day's low, (2) the distance from the previous day's high to the current day's low, or (3) the distance from the previous day's high to the current day's high.

Beta: Beta is not an absolute measure of volatility. It measures a stock's volatility relative to the market as a whole. Therefore, beta measures how a stock's price movement relates to changes in the entire stock market. Beta is often the subject of discussion among technical analysts. In order to calculate beta, the analyst must first obtain a measure of the broader market; the most common barometer is the S&P 500 index. Next, the market, or the S&P 500, is assigned a value of 1.00. Finally, the price changes of a stock are measured relative to the S&P 500. For example, a stock with a beta of 2.00 experiences price swings two times greater than those of the broader market.

Bollinger bands: John Bollinger is credited with the creation of Bollinger bands. Other technical analysts have put forth similar indicators known as standard deviation channels. Bollinger bands and trading channels are based on statistics and the mathematical concept known as the normal distribution. In the case of a stock price, the distribution is the stock's various prices over a period of time. It is the same price data that one uses to plot a stock chart. A normal distribution of a set of data (such as stock prices over a period of time) will have a tendency to cluster or center around an average value or mean. Bollinger bands are designed to measure the stock's tendency to move around that average or mean, in this case the stock's moving average. When a stock experiences high volatility, it will move sharply above or below its moving average and the bands (delineated by two lines) will widen. When a stock is trading within a narrow range, it will not deviate much from its moving average, and the bands will narrow. Mathematically, Bollinger bands are plotted two standard deviations above and below the moving average.

Standard deviation: A statistical measure of the variability of a set of numbers, or of a distribution. Statistical volatility is computed as the annualized standard deviation of closing stock prices over a fixed number of days. Therefore, when the variability of those stock prices, or the standard deviation, is high, statistical volatility will also be high.

Statistical volatility: There are many different ways to measure historical volatility, all designed to look at the volatility of an investment as it existed in the past. The most common method for options traders is statistical volatility, which is computed as the annualized standard deviation of past prices over a period of time (10, 30, or 90 days). Discussed in term of percentages, statistical volatility can be computed over different time frames, and the number of days under consideration will vary depending on the trader's trading time frame.

4

Trading Historical Volatility

Answers and Discussions

1. When prices are falling, fear and panic can overwhelm investors, which drives prices ____________.

   Answer: B—Lower

   Discussion: Investors respond in different ways to falling stock prices. Some view them as buying opportunities. Other times, however, falling stock prices cause investors to react emotionally. After all, shareholders generally want stock prices to rise. It makes them feel like savvy investors. Rising stock prices also give investors a sense of financial well-being and security. Falling stock prices, however, work in the opposite manner. When stock prices are falling, investors get a feeling of uncertainty. If the slide continues for a prolonged period of time, the feeling of uncertainty can give way to worry and nervousness. In the event of a sharp move lower—like a market crash—worry can turn into fear and sheer panic.

2. When prices are rising and the majority of investors are making money, optimism and greed drive prices ____________.

   Answer: A—Higher

   Discussion: When a stock or market is moving rapidly higher and investors are making money, there is a tendency for greed to take over and drive prices higher still. Greedy investors often make irrational decisions and focus too much on potential gains, and not enough on risk and volatility.

3. True or False: Historical volatility is computed using past stock prices and the Black-Scholes option pricing model.

Answer: False

Discussion: Historical volatility considers only past prices. The Black-Scholes model computes implied volatility and is discussed later in the book.

4. The most common method of measuring historical volatility is ____________.

   Answer: D—Statistical volatility

   Discussion: When option traders refer to historical or actual volatility, it is generally in reference to statistical volatility (SV), although SV is only one of the measures of historical volatility.

5. True or False: If a stock or an index fluctuates wildly in price, it is said to have high historical volatility, which could lead to lower option premiums.

   Answer: False

   Discussion: Option premiums rise when market participants—option traders, market makers, hedgers, and so on—expect greater volatility. When the historical volatility of a stock or index is high, there is a tendency for the market to drive option premiums higher as well. That is, it is natural to expect a stock or index that has high historical volatility to exhibit high volatility in the future, and the option premiums will reflect those expectations.

6. To make a determination as to what is normal for a particular stock or index, traders must consider historical volatility using ____________.

   Answer: C—Different time frames

   Discussion: Historical volatility is best viewed over time. Often, a stock or index will exhibit levels of volatility well above its normal range. Generally, however, a drop follows the high levels of historical volatility. The same is true during periods of extremely low levels of volatility. (i.e., a decline tends to be followed by an increase). Therefore, studying changes in statistical volatility for a stock or an asset can give the trader a better sense of what is normal, which will help identify deviations and subsequent trading opportunities.

7. Although historical volatility is always in a state of change, most stocks or indexes can be assigned a normal or average value. When volatility diverges greatly from that normal range, there is a tendency for it to revert back to that average. This is referred to as ____________.

   Answer: B—Reversion to the mean

   Discussion: The volatility of a stock or index tends to center around a normal or average value throughout long periods of time. In statistics, the average is also known as the mean. When volatility diverges greatly from that normal range, there is a tendency for it to revert back to that average, or mean. Therefore, if the volatility of a stock is low relative to its average over a long period of time, there is a tendency for the volatility to increase and revert back to its mean. Conversely, when the volatility of a stock or index is high relative to its long-term average, chances are greater that it will fall back toward the mean.

8. There are only two factors under consideration when computing moving averages: the stock price and ___________.

   Answer: B—Number of days

   Discussion: A moving average is simply the average of a stock or an index's price over a period of days. It considers closing prices and a fixed number of days. For example, traders often compute the 50-day moving average for stock prices.

9. True or False: Fifty- or 200-day moving averages are commonly used for studying short-term trends with regard to a stock or an index.

   Answer: False

   Discussion: The number of days used in the moving average generally depends on the trader's objectives. Short-term traders will generally use fewer days, for instance, 5, 10, or 13. Long-term traders frequently use 50-day and 200-day moving averages.

10. In general, a "buy" signal is triggered when the moving average begins an upward slope and the stock price closes ___________ it.

    Answer: A—Above

    Discussion: Moving averages trigger buy and sell signals when they cross over the stock price. A "buy" signal using moving averages occurs when the stock price closes above the moving average. The signal is more important if the moving average has already taken on an upward slope.

11. True or False: Generally, the shorter the time period used in the moving average, the greater the number of "buy" and "sell" signals.

    Answer: True

    Discussion: Short-term moving averages change direction more quickly than long-term moving averages. In addition, short-term moving averages will remain closer to the price on a stock chart (because the average is based on fewer days and, therefore, gives greater weight to the most recent price). As a result, there is a tendency for short-term moving averages to give more frequent, and less reliable, buy and sell signals.

12. ___________ is the price level at which a stock price attracts a significant amount of demand—the type of buying that can stop a downward slide in a stock price.

    Answer: A—Support

    Discussion: Support is a price area on a chart where a stock has shown the ability to bounce upward. Support levels can occur along trend lines at round numbers (such as $50 or $100 a share), or sometimes exist for no obvious reason. Nevertheless, when a stock has legitimate support, investor interest and demand for the stock are high at that level. Consequently, stocks will often rise off of support on increasing trading volume.

13. ____________ is a price level at which a stock or index has witnessed great amounts of supply and can no longer move higher.

    Answer: B—Resistance

    Discussion: Resistance areas often occur along trend lines or at round numbers such as $50, $75, or $100 a share. Stocks that meet resistance have a ceiling through which the stock price cannot rise. It is a sign of heavy supply at a specific price level. Only when that supply is absorbed can the resistance level be penetrated.

14. True or False: At first, it is best to use 9 days or 18 days for moving averages because nearly every software program out there has these set as defaults in their systems.

    Answer: False

    Discussion: Most software programs do use the 9- and 18-day moving averages, but these are not the best moving averages to use. First, software makers, not traders, have been responsible for the popularity of 9- and 18-day moving averages. Second, the 9- and 18-day moving averages will give too many unreliable signals. The better moving averages to use are the 50-day and 200-day.

15. During periods of high volatility, if the 50-day moving average pulls back to the 200-day moving average, this sets up a nice ____________ signal for the stock.

    Answer: A—Buy

    Discussion: Using the 50- and 200-day moving averages together can help provide accurate buy and sell signals. If the 50-day moving average pulls back to the 200-day moving average, it triggers a buy signal for the stock. A buy signal advises the trader to turn bullish and go long or buy the stock. The same holds true for the reverse, which creates a sell signal that advises the trader to turn bearish and go short or sell the stock.

16. True or False: When movement in the stock price is steady and less volatile, Bollinger bands tend to diverge or widen; when the movement of the stock or index begins to swing wildly and volatility rises, the bands tend to come together and become narrow.

    Answer: False

    Discussion: During periods of quiet trading or steady movement in a stock, Bollinger bands tend to become narrower. Conversely, when the movement of the stock or index begins to swing wildly and volatility rises, the bands tend to become wider or farther apart.

17. If a stock price moves above two standard deviations from its normal range, the stock is then considered ____________, and its price is due to fall back toward its moving average and correct.

    Answer: B—Overbought

Discussion: In addition to providing a gauge of a stock's volatility, Bollinger bands can be used as an overbought/oversold indicator. The top band lies two standard deviations above its moving average or normal range. When the stock rises up and penetrates the Bollinger band, it is a sign that the stock is overbought and due to head lower; when a stock falls through the lower Bollinger band, it is a sign that the stock is oversold and due to bounce.

18. Using Bollinger bands, how can you tell if the stock or index is ripe for a breakout?

    Answer: Look for Bollinger bands that are contracting to a point where the daily range of the market is close to touching both the upper band and the lower band.

    Discussion: This formation indicates that the market is tightening, much like the coiling of a spring. When a spring is coiled and then released, it propels itself in one direction with considerable momentum.

19. True or False: Historical volatility can be used to gauge when a stock is likely to get quiet or explosive by comparing 10-day to 90-day time frames. A very low 10/90 ratio suggests that the underlying stock is consolidating.

    Answer: True

    Discussion: Comparing volatility using different time frames can be extremely helpful to the technical trader. When the 10-day statistical volatility (SV) drops well below the 90-day statistical volatility, it suggests that the stock's volatility has experienced a sharp decline. This is generally the pattern when the stock is consolidating or moving within a narrow range.

20. The advantage of the ATR over statistical volatility is that it accounts for not only the closing price of a stock or option, but also ____________.

    Answer: C—The current highs and lows

    Discussion: ATR considers the close, high, and low prices of the day. It is computed as the average of the True Range (TR) over a fixed number of days. TR is computed as the greatest of:

    - The distance from the current day's high to the current day's low.
    - The distance from the previous day's high to the current day's low.
    - The distance from the previous day's high to the current day's high.

21. If a stock opens significantly ____________ than the previous day's closing level, it is known as a "gap up."

    Answer: A—Higher

    Discussion: A gap is an empty area on the stock chart. It can be created when a stock opens sharply higher than the previous day's high—a "gap up." When a stock opens at a price much lower than the previous day's low, it is referred to as a "gap down." For example, if a stock closes at $40 one day and opens at $35 on the next day, a gap down occurred.

22. True or False: When ATR rises to extreme highs, the path of least resistance is to the upside, and chances are the stock will rise even higher.

    Answer: False

    Discussion: Rising ATR is a sign that the stock's volatility is high. This generally occurs when the stock has made a sharp move lower. From that point, the stock should reverse course and head higher, but this does not always happen. Alternatively, high ATR can be a sign of high volatility on the upside, which often occurs just before a stock is set to reverse to the downside.

Media Assignment

Paper trading can be an eye-opening experience. It is relatively easy to do once the trader has access to quotes and charts, and it is simply a matter of keeping track of trades in a journal or an online portfolio service. Scan through the headlines, find moving stocks, and then study them using the various measures of historical volatility. Using the concepts from this chapter, the reader wants to identify stocks or indexes that have the strong potential of moving in one direction or the other. To paper trade correctly, note the current bid and ask for stocks or the last price for indexes, set a price target, and identify a time frame for the trade (30, 90, 180, etc. days). Try three or four new trades a week, print copies of the stock charts that caught your interest, and keep detailed records.

Vocabulary Definitions

Breakout: A sharp move higher or lower in a stock that signals its future direction. Breakouts often follow a move below a trend line or other support area, or above a trend line or other resistance zone. Legitimate breakouts are often accompanied by heavy trading volume.

Buy signals: Signals from technical indicators (such as trend lines, moving averages, or Bollinger bands) that suggest the stock or market is ready to move higher. In that case, the trader will assume a bullish position.

Gap down: An empty area on the stock chart caused when a stock opens at a price much lower than the previous day's low.

Gap up: An area on a stock chart that shows an empty space. It is caused when a stock opens the day at a price substantially higher from the previous day's high.

Moving average: An average of a set of variables such as stock prices over time. The term "moving" stems from the fact that as each new price is added, the first (or oldest) is deleted.

Normal range: Each stock price has a range that defines its normal activity. Generally, the normal range is quantified using moving averages. The volatility of a stock or index also has a normal range and is best viewed using a chart or graph.

Overbought condition: A situation in which a stock price has risen to unsustainable highs. Buyers can no longer push the price higher. Overbought stocks often have risen quite rapidly and then often suffer a short-term drop in price.

Oversold condition: A situation that describes a stock that has fallen rapidly in price and is set to bounce higher. Sellers have temporarily run out of supply.

Price consolidation: A period of time in which a stock or market moves sideways. Consolidation usually occurs after a significant trend higher or lower. During a period of consolidation, the stock or market is digesting its gains or losses. Volatility traders actively watch consolidating markets because they often precede breakouts.

Resistance: Resistance occurs at a price level where a large amount of selling takes place. As a result, a ceiling forms and the stock cannot rise any further. Resistance usually occurs at round numbers or along trend lines. Round numbers such as 25, 50, and 100 are often used as price targets. Therefore, many sellers are eager to get out at those prices. For that reason, when a stock hits one of those round numbers, traders have achieved their price target and begin unloading shares. The selling, in turn, will cause a halt to the stock's ascent. When this happens, it is known as resistance. Traders sometimes use trend lines as targets as well. Therefore, when a stock rises and approaches a downward sloping trend line, there is sometimes heavy selling, which causes resistance to higher prices. Finally, after a stock makes a precipitous fall, there are many investors who are anxious to get out of the stock. With each incremental gain, sellers surface and attempt to salvage anything they can. When this happens, the stock is said to have heavy overhead supply. Overhead supply is the amount of stock that sellers are holding and want to sell at a higher price. The term "overhead" is used because it will occur as the stock rises. For example, a trader might buy a stock for $40 with an objective of selling it at $50.

Reversion to the mean: Although volatility is always in a state of change, the volatility of stocks or indexes can be assigned a normal or average value. It is a value that the volatility of an index tends to center around throughout long periods of time. In statistics, the average is also known as the "mean." When volatility diverges greatly from that normal range, there is a tendency for it to eventually go back to that average, or mean. Therefore, if the volatility of a stock is low relative to its average over a long period of time, there is a tendency for the volatility to increase and revert back to its mean. On the other hand, when the volatility of a stock or index is high relative to its long-term average, chances are greater that it will fall back toward the mean.

Sell signals: Signals from technical indicators that suggest the stock or market is ready to move lower. Sell signals urge the trader to assume a bearish stance toward the stock or index.

Spike: An extremely high price point (e.g., an abnormally high bar) on a stock chart.

Support: A price level at which a stock price stops falling and begins to move higher. When the slide in a stock is halted at a specific price level on several occasions, it is said to have support at that level. It is a price point with unusually high investor interest or demand. Support can occur along trend lines, moving averages, or other important price levels.

True Range: A measure of a stock's daily volatility. It is computed as the greatest of: (1) the distance from the current day's high to the current day's low, (2) the distance from the previous day's high to the current day's low, or (3) the distance from the previous day's high to the current day's high.

5

The World of Stock Options

Answers and Discussions

1. True or False: Options traders are more concerned with historical volatility than implied volatility.

   Answer: False

   Discussion: Historical volatility and implied volatility are equally important to the options trader. Historical volatility reflects the past price movements of the underlying asset. Implied volatility is a measure of market expectations regarding the asset's future volatility. Implied volatility also tells whether options are cheap or expensive. Options traders must consider both historical and implied volatility prior to implementing trading strategies.

2. Name five things you can do using options as a trading instrument.

   Answers:

   1. Generate an income stream.
   2. Protect an existing stock position.
   3. Speculate on a move higher or lower in a stock.
   4. Position a trade to profit on a big swing in a stock, regardless of market direction.
   5. Profit from a move sideways in a stock.

3. Why are options called derivatives?

   Answer: The price of an option is *derived* from the underlying asset—from not only the price of the asset, but also the volatility of that stock or index.

Discussion: Derivative instruments are securities with values that fluctuate based on the value of another investment. The value of a stock option, for instance, will vary due primarily to changes in the stock.

4. Option prices on a high volatility stock will be ____________ than the equivalent option (with the same price) on a low volatility stock.

   Answer: B—Higher

   Discussion: All else being equal, stocks with higher actual volatility will command higher option premiums because their chances of rising above the strike price by expiration are greater. For example, a stock now trading for $25 a share that has been trading between $20 and $40 a share over the past six months will have a better chance of rising above $30 a share when compared to a similar stock (also trading for $25) that has been trading between $23 and $27 a share during the past six months. Therefore, options with a strike price of 30 will generally have higher option premiums in the first case because the odds of that option being in-the-money by expiration are greater.

5. True or False: Options offer opportunities to make profits regardless of whether the stock or index moves in either direction.

   Answer: True

   Discussion: Options can yield profits regardless of the direction of the stock or market. For example, puts increase in value when a stock falls.

6. In 1973, the ____________ formalized the trading of option contracts.

   Answer: B—Chicago Board Options Exchange (CBOE)

   Discussion: Prior to 1973, there was no formalized trading in options. Instead, prices were listed in newspapers and option traders negotiated among themselves. That changed in 1973, however, when the CBOE created the first organized options exchange.

7. The option contract specifies a price, known as the ____________, at which the stock can be bought or sold and a fixed date, called the ____________, by which the transaction must take place.

   Answer: A—Strike price/Expiration date

   Discussion: Options are generally discussed in terms of the underlying asset, the strike price of the option, and the expiration. Those three factors define the option contract. The strike price is the price at which the stock or index can be bought (calls) or sold (puts). The expiration date reflects the lifetime of the contract. Once the expiration date has passed, the contract ceases to exist and the option is worthless.

8. When puts and calls trade on one of the organized exchanges, they are referred to as ____________.

   Answer: A—Listed options

Discussion: The term "listed" simply refers to the fact that the options trade on one of the organized options exchanges—the Chicago Board Options Exchange, the International Securities Exchange, the American Stock Exchange, the Pacific Exchange, or the Philadelphia Stock Exchange.

9. True or False: The seller of an option is also known as a "writer."

   Answer: True

   Discussion: Writing an option is equivalent to selling an option. The two terms mean the same thing.

10. True or False: Option buyers must hold the option until it expires.

    Answer: False

    Discussion: An option buyer can exit a position anytime prior to expiration by selling the same number of contracts on the same underlying stock, with the same expiration dates and strike prices. In essence, closing the position involves selling an identical offsetting position. When placing the order, the trader must specify that he or she is "selling to close."

11. True or False: There is no difference between American- and European-style options.

    Answer: False

    Discussion: American-style options can be exercised at any time prior to expiration. European-style options can be exercised only at expiration. While most stock options settle American-style, most index options are European-style.

12. The call option gives the owner (the holder or buyer) the right to ____________ the underlying security at a specific price during a specific period of time.

    Answer: A—Buy

    Discussion: Calls give the holder the right to buy the underlying asset at the strike price of the option until the option expires. The call owner has the right to buy the underlying asset, but not the obligation to do so.

13. The put option gives the owner the right to ____________ a specific stock (underlying asset) at a specific price over a predetermined period of time.

    Answer: B—Sell

    Discussion: Puts give the holder the right to sell the underlying asset at the strike price of the option until the option expires. The put holder has the right to sell the underlying asset, but not the obligation to do so.

14. True or False: If a call is assigned and exercised, the call writer is obligated to deliver 100 shares of the underlying stock to the option buyer at the strike price.

    Answer: True

Discussion: Each option contract reflects 100 shares of the underlying stock. Until expiration, for each option contract sold, a call writer has the obligation to sell 100 shares of stock at the strike price of the option if the option is assigned and exercised. The position can be closed prior to expiration, however, through an offsetting transaction (i.e., buying the same number of calls of the same contract).

15. True or False: If a put is assigned, the put writer is obligated to buy 100 shares of the underlying stock from the option buyer at the strike price.

    Answer: True

    Discussion: For each put contract sold, the put seller has the obligation to buy 100 shares of stock at the strike price of the option until expiration if the option is assigned and exercised. After expiration, the put seller no longer has that obligation.

16. An in-the-money call option has a strike price ____________ the stock price.

    Answer: B—Below

    Discussion: In-the-money (ITM) describes an option with intrinsic value. In the case of a call, if the strike price is below the current market price for the stock and the call is exercised, the stock can be sold in the market at the current market price for a profit.

17. An out-of-the-money put option has a strike price ____________ the stock price.

    Answer: B—Below

    Discussion: Out-of-the-money (OTM) refers to an option with no intrinsic value. Therefore, there is no potential gain possible from exercising the option. For a put, it describes a situation where the strike price is below the current market price of the stock because the put owner would not profit from selling the stock at the strike price when it is less than the stock's current market price.

18. Any option contract can be discussed in terms of specifications regarding ____________.

    Answer: E—All of the above [the type (put or call), the underlying stock or index, the strike price, and the expiration month]

    Discussion: Options are contracts or agreements between two parties. Each contract has specific terms and can be defined by these four variables.

19. Each stock is assigned to one of three quarterly expiration cycles. Name the months in these cycles.

    Answers:

    Cycle 1: January, April, July, October

    Cycle 2: February, May, August, November

    Cycle 3: March, June, September, December

Discussion: All options are assigned an expiration cycle that includes four months, which are spaced evenly at three-month intervals. In addition, option expirations generally include the two nearest months. Therefore, in January, a stock option on the March expiration cycle will have options expiring in January, February, March, June, September, and December. In this case, January is referred to as the "front month" contract.

20. True or False: Expiration occurs on the first Saturday of the expiration month.

    Answer: False

    Discussion: Expiration occurs on the *third* Saturday of the expiration month. It is important to note that the last day for trading is the preceding day, Friday.

21. The ____________ of the underlying asset is the most important factor in determining the value of an option.

    Answer: C—Price

    Discussion: There are a number of factors that can influence the price of an option such as time left until expiration and changes in implied volatility. The most important factor, however, is the price of the underlying asset.

22. Why are options referred to as "wasting assets"?

    Answer: Options are sometimes called wasting assets because they lose value as time passes.

    Discussion: Since options are contracts with fixed expiration dates, their values diminish over time, a phenomenon known as "time decay."

23. True or False: Moneyness describes the relationship between the price of an underlying asset and the price of an option on that same underlying asset.

    Answer: False

    Discussion: Moneyness describes the relationship between the price of an underlying asset relative to the *strike price* of an option on that same underlying asset. Options are either in-the-money, at-the-money, or out-of-the-money.

24. The difference between the strike price and the underlying asset's price is known as ____________

    Answer: C—Intrinsic value

    Discussion: Whether or not an option has intrinsic value depends on the relationship between the strike price of the option and the actual price of the underlying asset. For example, a call that has a strike price below the current market price of the underlying asset has intrinsic value, which is computed as the stock price minus the strike price. A call option with a strike price above the current market price of the stock has zero intrinsic value. Basically, option contracts consist of intrinsic value plus time value. When an option has zero intrinsic value, it consists of only time value.

25. True or False: At-the-money (ATM) options and out-of-the-money (OTM) options have zero intrinsic value.

    Answer: True

    Discussion: Only in-the-money options are worth anything at expiration and thus have positive intrinsic value. This is true of both puts and calls.

26. The ____________ is the safety net behind the options market and ensures that investors are not at risk of a financial collapse on the part of a broker, an exchange, or other options market participant.

    Answer: C—Options Clearing Corporation (OCC)

    Discussion: The Options Clearing Corporation was founded in 1973. Today, it is the world's largest clearing organization for financial derivative instruments. Operating under the jurisdiction of the Securities and Exchange Commission (SEC), the Options Clearing Corporation is considered a safety net behind all U.S. exchange-listed securities options. The OCC also issues put and call options on stocks, indexes, and other underlying assets. The major options exchanges—the American Stock Exchange, the Chicago Board Options Exchange, the Pacific Exchange, the Philadelphia Stock Exchange, and the International Securities Exchange—share equal ownership in the Options Clearing Corporation (www.optionsclearing.com).

27. True or False: An option with only three weeks remaining in its life will see a much faster rate of time decay than an equivalent option with 12 months of life remaining.

    Answer: True

    Discussion: Time decay is not linear. Instead, time decay becomes greater as expiration approaches. Therefore, all else being equal, the option that is nearer to expiration will see a faster rate of time decay.

28. Name five things that influence an option's premium.

    Answers:

    1. Time left until expiration.
    2. The underlying asset's volatility.
    3. The prevailing interest rate.
    4. Whether the underlying asset pays a dividend.
    5. The option strike price in relation to the current underlying asset price.

    Discussion: A number of factors have an impact on the value of an option. The price of the underlying asset is the most important, but there are others. Option traders want to keep in mind the impact of changes in implied volatility and time decay on their positions. Interest rates and dividends, in some cases, can also influence the value of an option, but are not as important as the other three factors.

29. True or False: The higher the volatility of the underlying asset, the higher the option premium.

    Answer: True

    Discussion: All else being equal, stocks with higher volatility will have higher option premiums because there is a greater chance that the stock price will rise above (call) or fall below (put) the strike price by expiration. See the discussion in Chapter 4, Question 5.

30. True or False: The theoretical value of an option derived from any option pricing model will not always be equal to its value in the marketplace.

    Answer: True

    Discussion: When using an option pricing model to solve for the price of an option, the result is known as the "theoretical value." The primary reason for the difference between the theoretical price of an option and its actual price in the marketplace stems from different assumptions regarding volatility. That is, the volatility percentage used to compute the theoretical price of an option is sometimes different from the current level of volatility implied in the option's price. To find the current level of volatility implied in the option's price, the strategist uses the option pricing model along with the current option price to solve for implied volatility. Therefore, option pricing models can be used to (1) solve for the option's price using a given level of volatility, or (2) solve for implied volatility given the option's current price in the market. In the first case, the result, called the theoretical value of an option, can be different from the current value of the option in the marketplace.

31. If open interest on the August IBM 75 call is 3,020, what does this mean?

    Answer: It tells us that there have been 3,020 options bought or sold on the August IBM 75 call.

    Discussion: Open interest refers to all open positions on a contract. Each option contract has its own level of open interest. The greater the figure, the greater the liquidity and trading activity associated with the option contract. Open interest does not tell, however, whether the open contracts are purchases or sales.

32. True or False: In order to trade options, all you have to do is open a brokerage account.

    Answer: False

    Discussion: In order to trade options, one must first open an account *and* obtain approval to trade options. The business of buying and selling options for customers is under strict supervision of federal regulatory agencies. For that reason, brokerage firms must ensure that trading options is suitable for each customer by assessing the individual's total financial situation. In addition to a new account form, the aspiring options trader must complete an options approval form, which helps the brokerage firm determine whether options are an appropriate financial instrument for each particular individual to trade.

33. True or False: Index options settle for cash, and not shares.

    Answer: True

    Discussion: Unlike stock options, which settle for shares, index options settle for cash. The amount of cash is based on the difference between the strike price of the option and the actual value of the index at the time the option is exercised.

Media Assignment

Implied volatility (IV) is one of the most important, and most overlooked, aspects of options trading. It is the amount of volatility that an option is expected to exhibit in the future and is expressed as a percentage. In addition, implied volatility is computed directly from the option's market price and an option pricing model such as the one developed by Fischer Black and Myron Scholes (the Black-Scholes model). Each option contract will have a unique level of implied volatility. When options on the same stock have different levels of IV, it is known as a volatility skew—a concept taken up in Chapter 10. For now, however, the reader should have a means for obtaining implied volatility information for any option. This can be done using an option pricing model that is available on a number of different web sites or in options trading software packages. In order to do so, the model requires the following inputs: the option's price, the strike price of the option, and the time to expiration, along with the price of the underlying asset (accounting for dividends) and the prevailing interest rate (T-bill).

Implied volatility reflects not past volatility of an asset, but rather market expectations concerning what the asset's volatility is likely to be going forward. The drawback to using models, however, is the fact that entering all of the pertinent variables can be time-consuming. In addition, using a model does not provide historical information concerning past levels of IV.

Alternatively, the reader can subscribe to a service such as the Optionetics.com Platinum site for a fee. For the active options trader, a subscription fee is well worth the price. Among other things, Optionetics.com Platinum allows traders to chart implied volatility for stock and index options. This provides a means for viewing whether IV is high or low relative to the past. In addition, there is no need for option calculators. The implied volatility information is already computed. Without a subscription to Optionetics.com Platinum, however, traders can still obtain valuable implied volatility information from Optionetics.com at no cost. Specifically, there is a free ranker that sorts options using a number of different factors. For example, it is possible to rank stocks based on whether the options are cheap (low implied volatility) or expensive (high IV).

The free ranker is accessible from the Optionetics.com home page. Look through the lists and study some of the stocks that have cheap or expensive options.

For example, after creating a list of expensive options, click on the stock's name and symbol. Doing so will take the user to charts of the stock and the option's implied volatility. Examine a group of stocks and notice how the IV changes when the stock rises or falls. Also, for those stocks with expensive options, search through the financial press to see if there is a news story that helps explain why IV is high. Often, options are expensive because traders expect volatility to increase going forward, and that is generally due to a news event concerning the company and/or industry. As usual, keep notes on your findings in your trading journal.

Vocabulary List

American-style options: Options that can be exercised anytime prior to expiration. Stock options settle American-style.

Assignment: The act of fulfilling the obligation of the option under the terms of the contract. When assigned, the call writer must sell the stock at the strike price. When the put seller faces assignment, he or she must buy the stock at the strike price.

At-the-money (ATM): An option with a strike price equal to the price of the underlying asset.

Black-Scholes model: An option pricing model developed by the Nobel prize-winning work of Fischer Black and Myron Sholes in the early 1970s. In order to use the model, a number of variables are required: the strike price of the option, and the time to expiration, along with the price of the underlying asset (accounting for dividends), the prevailing interest rate (T-bill), and either the option's price or volatility. That is, the model can be used to solve for either a theoretical price or the current implied volatility.

Call: An option contract that gives the owner the right, but not the obligation, to buy the underlying asset at a predetermined price (strike price) for a specific period of time (until expiration). Calls increase in value as the underlying asset moves higher.

Closing transaction: A trade that is used to offset an open position in a trading account. For example, a trader removes a long position in XYZ 50 calls by selling an equal number of XYZ 50 calls in a closing transaction. Also known as selling to close. Similarly, a short position in XYZ 50 calls is offset through a buying to close transaction.

Derivative: A security whose value fluctuates based on the value of another investment. The value of a stock option, for instance, will vary due primarily to changes in the underlying stock.

Dividends: A percentage of a corporation's profits that is passed on to shareholders. The amount of dividends a shareholder receives is based on the number of shares held. Dividends are paid quarterly.

Downside move: A drop in the value of an investment security.

European-style options: Options that can be exercised only at expiration. Most indexes settle European-style.

Exercise: Invoking the right granted under the terms of the option contract. For a call holder, exercise involves buying the stock at the strike price from the call seller. The put holder exercises his or her option by selling the stock at the strike price of the option at or before expiration.

Expiration: The point in time when an option contract ceases to exist. For stock options, expiration is the third Saturday of the expiration month.

Implied volatility: Implied volatility is the amount of volatility an option is expected to exhibit in the future and is computed directly using an option pricing model such as Black-Scholes. The model requires the following inputs: the option's price, the strike price of the option, and the time to expiration, along with the price of the underlying asset (accounting for dividends) and the prevailing interest rate (T-bill). Implied volatility reflects not past volatility of an asset, but rather market expectations concerning what the asset's volatility is likely to be going forward.

In-the-money (ITM): An option that has intrinsic value. A call option has intrinsic value when the strike price of the option is below the current market price of the stock. A put option is ITM when the strike price is above the current market price of the stock.

Intrinsic value: A measure of the value of an option based on the difference between its strike price and the current market price of the underlying asset. For stock options, a call has intrinsic value when the strike price of the option is below the current market price of the stock. A put option has intrinsic value when the strike price is above the current market price of the stock.

LEAPS: Long-term equity anticipation securities are long-term option contracts with expirations as much as two and a half years out. LEAPS expire in January. For example, in May 2002, the 2004 LEAPS expire on the third Saturday of January 2004.

Opening transaction: A trade that adds a new position to a trader's account. For example, a new purchase of XYZ 50 calls is an opening position. At the same time, a new sale of XYZ 50 calls (as in a covered call) is also an opening transaction.

Open interest: Open interest refers to all open positions on a contract. Each option contract has its own level of open interest. The greater the figure, the greater the liquidity and trading activity associated with the option contract. Open interest does not tell, however, whether the open contracts have been bought or sold.

Options Clearing Corporation (OCC): The world's largest clearing organization for financial derivatives instruments. Founded in 1973 and operating under the jurisdiction of the Securities and Exchange Commission (SEC), the Options Clearing Corporation is considered the safety net behind all U.S. exchange-listed securities options. The OCC also issues put and call options on stocks, indexes, and other underlying assets. The major option exchanges—the American Stock Exchange, the Chicago Board Options Exchange, the Pacific Exchange, the Philadelphia Stock Exchange, and the International Securities Exchange—share equal ownership in the Options Clearing Corporation.

Out-of-the-money (OTM): Options that have no intrinsic value. A call with a strike price above the current market price of the underlying asset is considered OTM. Conversely, a put with a strike price below the current price of the underlying security is out-of-the-money.

Put: An option contract that gives the owner the right, but not the obligation, to sell the underlying asset at a predetermined price (strike price) for a specific period of time (until expiration). Puts increase in value as the underlying asset moves lower.

Time decay: The drop in the value of an option due to the fact that it has a fixed expiration date. As the expiration date approaches, the option loses time value—its time value decays.

Time value: The amount by which the value of an option exceeds its intrinsic value.

Underlying asset (security): The investment vehicle that the option holder has the right to buy (call holder) or sell (put holder) based on the terms of the option contract.

Wasting assets: Investment vehicles that lose value as time elapses. Options, which have fixed expiration dates and lose value as time passes, are an example.

Writer: The seller of an option.

6

Implied Volatility

Answers and Discussions

1. Implied volatility is expressed as a percentage and is derived by using ____________.

   Answer: D—An options pricing model

   Discussion: Implied volatility is computed using the Black-Scholes or other pricing model. These models require several inputs, including the option's expiration date, the strike price of the option, the price of the underlying asset, the prevailing interest rate, any dividends paid, and the current option's price. The model then solves for the option's implied volatility, which is expressed as a percentage. Alternatively, a volatility percentage can be entered into the model, which will then solve for the option's (theoretical) price.

2. True or False: Implied volatility indicates to the option strategist whether options are cheap or expensive.

   Answer: True

   Discussion: Implied volatility will fluctuate as expectations regarding the underlying asset's future volatility change. For instance, if market players (option traders, hedgers, market makers, etc.) expect shares of XYZ company to exhibit higher volatility going forward, option premiums will rise. The rise is due to an increase in IV.

3. When two options on the same stock have vastly different implied volatilities, it is known as volatility ____________.

   Answer: D—Skew

   Discussion: Each option contract has a unique level of volatility. Therefore, two options on the same stock but with different expiration dates and/or strike prices can have different levels of IV. When this happens, it is referred to as a skew. Large volatility skews create trading opportunities.

4. True or False: Volatility never changes, and remains the same over time.

   Answer: False

   Discussion: Volatility is always in a state of flux and can change from one minute to the next.

5. Name three things that impact implied volatility.

   Answers:

   1. A stellar or unexpected profit announcement
   2. News of a takeover
   3. Accounting irregularities

   Discussion: A number of different factors can cause implied volatility to jump higher. Basically, anytime there is reason to believe that an underlying asset will exhibit wider price swings in the future, it is reasonable to expect IV to move higher. Expectations of a strong earnings report, takeover rumors, or worries concerning accounting irregularities can all cause implied volatility spikes.

6. True or False: When implied volatility rises, options become cheap; when implied volatility falls, the option premiums rise.

   Answer: False

   Discussion: Rising implied volatility causes option prices to rise or become more expensive. Falling IV results in lower option premiums. Therefore, all else being equal, when implied volatility on an option is high, it is better to sell that option. When IV is low, the option is more suitable for buying.

7. Dividends are periodic payments a company makes to its ____________.

   Answer: D—Shareholders

   Discussion: Dividends are a percentage of a corporation's profits that is passed on to stockholders. The amount of dividends a shareholder receives is based on the number of shares held. Dividends are paid quarterly to existing shareholders.

8. True or False: The impact of dividends will not be equal on all call options.

   Answer: True

   Discussion: The impact of dividends on call options will depend on the size of the dividend. For instance, the call options on a stock trading for $20 a share and paying $1 in dividends will have a greater impact from the dividend than a stock trading for $100 a share and paying only 25 cents in dividends.

9. Implied volatility gives a sense of what traders and market makers believe the volatility of the stock will be in the ____________.

Answer: A—Future

Discussion: Since implied volatility is derived from the actual option prices in the marketplace, it reflects expectations regarding the future. By measuring IV, you discover the level of volatility currently priced into the option—a sign of what market participants anticipate going forward.

10. True or False: In the case of a takeover rumor, the call options generally see growing investor interest and, as a result, the implied volatility will rise.

    Answer: True

    Discussion: Takeover rumors often lead to IV spikes. Basically, the takeover talk fuels expectations that the stock will make a significant move higher in the near future, and the option premiums rise to reflect the anticipation of higher volatility going forward.

11. True or False: Higher interest rates mean lower option prices, while lower interest rates mean higher premiums.

    Answer: False

    Discussion: Although subject to some debate, most financial theorists hold that higher interest rates lead to higher option premiums and lower interest rates cause option premiums to fall.

12. The first step in determining whether options are cheap or expensive is to compare ____________.

    Answer: B—Implied volatility over time

    Discussion: The implied volatility of an option is always changing. There are times when it is high and other times when it is low, but there is generally a customary or normal range. In addition, each option contract will have a unique level of implied volatility. Therefore, to truly understand, at any given point in time, whether IV is high or low, it is important to compare the current readings of each individual option to the levels that have existed in the past.

13. CBOE Volatility Index, or VIX, provides real-time information regarding the implied volatility of ____________.

    Answer: D—S&P 100 (OEX) index options

    Discussion: The Chicago Board Options Exchange created the CBOE Volatility Index in 1983 as a way of viewing real-time information concerning the implied volatility in the market. At the time, the S&P 100 index options were the most actively traded, and therefore VIX was based on the IV of the options on that index.

14. If the theoretical value of an option is computed using the statistical volatility of the stock equal to 15%, but the implied volatility of the option is 25%, the market price of the option will be ____________ the theoretical value.

Answer: B—Higher than

Discussion: The theoretical value of an option is computed using an option pricing model and an assumed level of volatility. The level of volatility used is often statistical volatility (SV). However, if the SV is significantly below the current implied volatility in the market, the theoretical value will be too low. For example, if the option strategist computes the option price using an SV of 10%, but the market is currently pricing in higher volatility (say, implied volatility equals 20%), the theoretical value will be below the actual market price of the option.

15. The protective put provides ____________ on a long stock position just in case the stock takes a dive.

Answer: D—Insurance

Discussion: Puts increase in value as a stock moves lower. In addition, a put gives the owner the right to sell a stock at a predetermined price prior to expiration. Therefore, puts are often used to insure a stock in the event of a downside move. If the stock price falls, the owner can sell the stock at the price specified by the option contract. The degree of protection, therefore, will be determined by the strike price of the put.

16. True or False: When stock prices are falling, implied volatility tends to rise; but when stock prices are rising, implied volatility tends to fall.

Answer: True

Discussion: Since implied volatility reflects expectations regarding future volatility, it is not unusual to see it rise when the price of the underlying asset falls. Basically, market participants associate falling stock prices with greater volatility. Therefore, the sense that a falling stock is more volatile than a rising stock will often cause implied volatility to rise when the stock falls (and IV to fall when the stock advances). The degree to which IV rises often depends on the extent of the stock's decline. That is, a violent move lower in a stock is likely to cause implied volatility to rise faster than a gradual decline.

17. The covered call is also known as a ____________.

Answer: E—Buy-write

Discussion: The covered call is sometimes called a buy-write because the investor is buying the stock and writing, or selling, the calls. That way, if the call is assigned, the call seller already has the shares to deliver to the call buyer.

18. In a covered call, one call is sold for every ____________ shares of stock that are held.

Answer: D—100

Discussion: Since one option contract equals 100 shares of stock, the covered call involves the sale of one call for every 100 shares of stock owned. In that way, if the stock is called, the investor has enough shares to fulfill the assignment.

19. True or False: In the covered call strategy, the owner of stock is also a seller, or writer, of calls.

    Answer: True

    Discussion: The covered call involves the sale of calls against stock that is already owned. The purchase of the stock and the sale of the calls can take place simultaneously, or the calls can be sold against stock that is already held in a portfolio.

20. True or False: The covered call is best used when the investor is moderately bearish on a stock.

    Answer: False

    Discussion: The covered call is best used when the strategist is moderately bullish on a stock because it generally yields the best results when the stock moves slightly higher in price.

21. Calculate the maximum risk and reward as well as the breakeven for each of the following trades:

    Protective Put: Buy 100 Shares XYZ @ 40 and Buy 1 Oct XYZ 40 Put @ 4

    Strategy = Buy 100 shares of stock and buy 1 ATM put option

    Maximum Reward = Unlimited as the stock moves higher

    Maximum Risk = (Stock price – strike price) + put premium = [(40 – 40) + 4] × 100 = $400

    Breakeven = Stock price + put option premium = 40 + 4 = 44

    Covered Call: Buy 100 Shares XYZ @ 37.50 and Sell 1 Oct XYZ 40 Call @ 3

    Strategy = Sell an OTM call with 30 to 45 days to expiration against 100 long shares of stock

    Maximum Reward = Credit from call premium + (strike price – stock price) = 3 + (40 – 37.50) × 100 = $550

    Maximum Risk = Limited to the downside beyond the breakeven all the way to zero

    Breakeven = Stock price – put premium = 37.50 – 3 = 34.50

Media Assignment

How are your trades working out? After reading the media assignment for this chapter, the trader should have added a number of positions to his or her paper trading journal. The trades include protective puts and covered calls. In order to establish the positions, the reader was encouraged to use the free options ranker available on the Optionetics.com home page. We will see in later chapters other strategies that offer better risks and rewards than the covered call and protective put. But for now, three important lessons from the assignment are:

1. Learn to identify cheap (low implied volatility) and expensive (high IV) options.
2. Structure theoretical trades using both stocks and options.
3. Monitor the prices and implied volatility changes over time.

Throughout the next few weeks, the trader should revisit the trades from this chapter and ask a series of questions. Has the situation developed as anticipated? Are the stocks moving in the right direction? Has implied volatility of the options been rising, falling, or staying the same? Did any unexpected events trigger a sharp increase in implied volatility? What has been the total return or loss? Would simply owning the stock have provided better returns? These questions are not designed to encourage the use of the covered call or protective put, but rather to help the reader get a feel for changes in stock prices, option premiums, and implied volatility in the real world. There simply is no way to get a sense of how the three interrelate without using real or live prices.

Vocabulary Definitions

Buy-write: Another way of referring to the covered call.

CBOE Volatility Index (VIX): A measure of the implied volatility of S&P 100, or OEX, options. VIX is often called the market's "fear gauge" because it rises when market participants become nervous and begin actively hedging portfolios with OEX puts.

Covered call: The covered call involves the sale of calls against stock that is already owned. The purchase of the stock and the sale of the call can take place simultaneously, or the calls can be sold against stock that is already held in a portfolio. For investors, the covered call is considered a way of generating income from a stock holding. It is also considered less risky than simply owning the stock because the premium earned from selling the call offsets some of the cost of the stock. However, it is not a risk-free trade, and losses can result when the stock falls.

Delta: The point change in an option for every point change in the underlying asset. For example, a stock option with a delta of .50 will increase 50 cents for every $1 per share increase in the underlying stock price.

Gamma: A Greek tool that measures the changes in delta for each point change in the underlying asset. A high gamma means that the delta of a position will change rapidly for a relatively small movement in the underlying asset.

The greeks: Risk measurement tools that are computed using option pricing models. Each risk measurement has been assigned a Greek letter. Examples include theta, delta, and gamma.

Hedge: To protect from a downside move in an underlying asset. For example, puts are often used to hedge the downside move in a stock.

Implied volatility: Computed using the Black-Scholes or other pricing model, implied volatility is derived using current option prices in the market. To solve for implied volatility, option pricing models require several inputs including the option's expiration date, the strike price of the option, the price of the underlying asset, the prevailing interest rate, any dividends paid, and the current option's price. The model then solves for the option's implied volatility, which is expressed as a percentage. Alternatively, a volatility percentage can be entered into the model, which will then solve for the option's theoretical price.

Leverage: The use of capital to control a larger position in an underlying asset. For example, investors often borrow money through brokers (by using margin) to buy stocks. Doing so requires that a percentage of the money borrowed be deposited in a trading account. The deposit is a percentage of the total cost of the trade (the deposited funds plus the borrowed funds) and is used as leverage. Options are considered to be leveraged investments because they allow owners to control a relatively large amount of stock with relatively little trading capital.

Protective put: The protective put combines the purchase of the underlying security and the purchase of an ATM or OTM put option. For investors, the protective put is considered a way to protect the long stock position from a decline. Maximum profit is unlimited as the stock moves higher. Maximum risk is limited to the stock price minus the strike price plus the put premium.

Skew: When two or more option contracts on the same underlying asset with different strike prices and/or expiration dates have vastly different levels of implied volatility. A number of options trading strategies are designed to take advantage of various kinds of volatility skews.

Stock split: A split is the process of lowering a stock price by increasing the number of a company's shares outstanding. For example, a company whose stock is trading for $100 a share and with 100,000 shares outstanding might institute a two-for-one split. After the split, the stock will trade for $50 a share and there will be 200,000 shares outstanding. While some investors view splits as a favorable sign for the company and buy shares on the news, in practice it is nothing more than an accounting change. It adds no value to the company—just increases or decreases the number of shares.

Theta: The Greek measurement for the time decay of an option.

Vega: Term for the amount by which the price of an option changes when the volatility changes. Also referred to as the volatility of an option.

7

VIX and Other Sentiment Indicators

Answers and Discussions

1. ____________ different exchanges list options.

   Answer: C—Five

   Discussion: Today, options trade primarily on five exchanges: the American Stock Exchange, the Pacific Exchange, the Philadelphia Stock Exchange, the Chicago Board Options Exchange, and the International Securities Exchange.

2. True or False: When the mood toward stocks and the market turns pessimistic, most investors will lean toward caution and buy put options for downside protection.

   Answer: True

   Discussion: Puts are generally purchased to bet on the downside move in a stock. In addition, puts are often used to hedge stock holdings against a move lower. For that reason, when investors become predominantly bearish or pessimistic toward the stock market, put activity tends to increase.

3. When investors turn optimistic regarding stocks and the U.S. market, speculative activity will lead to ____________ in call buying.

   Answer: A—An increase

   Discussion: Many call buyers are speculators betting that a stock or index will make a move higher. Often during bull markets speculative activity can become quite high. As a result, call buying will be high as well.

4. Looking at the options market to glean information about investor psychology is also known as ____________.

   Answer: C—Sentiment analysis

   Discussion: Sentiment analysis is the process of studying the prevailing market psychology to determine whether investors are primarily bullish or bearish. It is an effort in contrary thinking and a search for extremes. When the majority of investors are bullish, they cannot all be correct, and the contrarian will turn negative or bearish. Conversely, if the trading crowd is mostly bearish, the contrary thinker will assume that their pessimism will give way to a market rally.

5. True or False: When the crowd is predominantly pessimistic regarding the market, the contrarian will become optimistic.

   Answer: True

   Discussion: The contrary thinker believes that the investing public is generally wrong at the major turning points in the market. That means excessive pessimism is a reason to turn bullish on the market.

6. The key to using sentiment analysis successfully lies in identifying ____________.

   Answer: C—Extremes

   Discussion: Sentiment analysis is a search for extremes. The public is not wrong all of the time, but generally on the wrong side of the market during major turning points. Therefore, the best time to bet against the majority view is when bullish or bearish sentiment has reached an extreme.

7. ____________ has become the number one gauge of market volatility available today.

   Answer: C—VIX

   Discussion: The CBOE Volatility Index, or VIX, was created by the Chicago Board Options Exchange in the early 1980s and has become the most widely used measure of market volatility. It is the market's so-called "fear gauge." During times of market turbulence, VIX will rise. When VIX falls to low levels, investor bullishness or complacency is suggested.

8. During times of uncertainty and market turmoil, VIX will ____________ to reflect greater expectations regarding future volatility.

   Answer: A—Rise

   Discussion: The CBOE Volatility Index, or VIX, reflects the implied volatility currently priced into S&P 100 index options. During times of uncertainty, market participants (option traders, hedgers, market makers, etc.) begin to price in expectations of greater volatility going forward by increasing the premiums afforded to OEX options. The increase in premiums is due to a rise in implied volatility—exactly what VIX measures best.

9. VIX is often referred to as ____________.

   Answer: D—The fear gauge

   Discussion: The CBOE Volatility Index is sometimes called the fear gauge because it tends to rise when investors become nervous, anxious, or fearful.

10. True or False: During the market crash in October 1987, VIX hit a record high of 173%, which has since been surpassed only by the mini-crash of 1989.

    Answer: False

    Discussion: VIX has never risen above the levels of October 1987, not even during the mini-crash of 1989.

11. True or False: S&P 500 index options and Dow Jones Industrial Average index options settle European-style.

    Answer: True

    Discussion: Most index options settle European-style—with a few exceptions including the Amex Oil Index (XOI), the PHLX Semiconductor Index (SOX), and the PHLX Gold and Silver Mining Index (XAU)—and therefore can be exercised only at expiration. In contrast, most stock options settle American-style and can be exercised at any time prior to expiration.

12. The proliferation of a large number of ____________ has been the most important factor behind the drop in OEX option trading.

    Answer: D—Other index option contracts

    Discussion: Index option trading dates back to 1983 and the Chicago Board Options Exchange's launch of options on the S&P 100 index. Since that time, however, a number of other index products have emerged. For example, one of the most actively traded option contracts today is the Nasdaq 100 QQQ. It is an exchange-traded fund (ETF) that tracks the performance of the Nasdaq 100 Index. It and a number of other indexes have been largely responsible for the decline in OEX trading.

13. True or False: VXN was created to track the implied volatility of the popular NDX options contract.

    Answer: True

    Discussion: The Nasdaq 100 Volatility Index, or VXN, was developed by the Chicago Board Options Exchange. It is similar to VIX, but measures the implied volatility on Nasdaq 100 Index (NDX) options, instead of the OEX.

14. True or False: The VIX and VXN tend to move in opposite directions most of the time.

    Answer: False

    Discussion: VIX and VXN both measure the implied volatility of index options, the OEX and NDX. As a result, they move in a similar manner. However, since the Nasdaq 100 Index (NDX) is the more volatile of the two indexes, VXN is usually higher than VIX.

15. Match the index options to the correct ticker symbol in Table 7.2.

Table 7.2 Match Index Option to Ticker Symbol—Answer

Index	*Tickers*
Nasdaq 100 Index Trust	QQQ
Mini-Nasdaq 100	MNX
S&P 100	OEX
S&P 500	SPX
Dow Jones Industrial Average	DJX

16. The ____________ is a composite measure of implied volatility on QQQ options.

Answer: B—QQV

Discussion: Trading under the ticker symbol QQV, the QQQ Volatility Index was launched on January 23, 2001. The index is designed to measure the implied volatility on the popular Nasdaq 100 QQQ (QQQ) options. The name of the investment was changed from the Nasdaq 100 Index Trust to the Nasdaq 100 QQQ. The volatility index (QQV) is known as the QQQ Volatility Index.

17. Name two differences between the MNX and the QQQ.

Answers:

1. The Mini-Nasdaq 100, MNX, settles for cash, while the QQQ settles for shares.
2. The MNX is equal to one-tenth the value of the NDX, while QQQ is designed to equal one-fortieth of the NDX.

Discussion: Like the Dow Jones Industrial Average and the Nasdaq Composite index, the Mini-Nasdaq 100 is a cash-based index. It serves two purposes. It can be used as a benchmark to gauge the performance of the Nasdaq 100 (NDX), which includes 100 of the largest nonfinancial companies trading on the Nasdaq. Additionally, options traders can participate in the rise and fall of the Nasdaq 100 through MNX options. Since it is a cash-based index, however, it cannot be bought or sold. There are no shares available for purchase. The Nasdaq 100 QQQ is similar to the MNX in that its value is also derived from the Nasdaq 100. However, while the Mini-Nasdaq 100 is equal to $^1/_{10}$th of the NDX, the Nasdaq 100 QQQ is designed to equal $^1/_{40}$th. In addition, the Nasdaq 100 QQQ is an exchange-traded fund. Therefore, in addition to QQQ options, investors can participate in the rise or fall of the Nasdaq 100 by buying or selling QQQ shares.

18. True or False: VIX, VXN, and QQV tend to rise when investors become complacent toward the outlook for the market and expect volatility to fall.

    Answer: False

    Discussion: VIX, VXN, and QQV tend to rise when investors become negative or bearish toward the market. Since all three measure the implied volatility of options, they tend to increase when market participants expect market volatility to increase going forward.

19. A high VIX means ___________ stocks (not options); but a low VIX urges ___________.

    Answer: C—Buy/Caution

    Discussion: The adage among option traders is, "When VIX is high, it's time to buy (stocks); when VIX is low, it is time to go (or sell stocks)." In this way, it is used as a contrary indicator because high VIX reflects growing levels of bearishness or pessimism, but a low VIX suggests bullishness or complacency.

20. True or False: It is rare to see VIX dip below the historical volatility of the OEX.

    Answer: True

    Discussion: The CBOE Volatility Index, which measures the implied volatility of OEX options, has historically remained above the actual volatility of the OEX.

21. True or False: Most option traders are either hedgers or speculators, and their strategies are limited to the straight purchase of puts and calls.

    Answer: True

    Discussion: The majority of option trades reflect the trading activity of either speculators, who are predominantly call buyers, or large traders attempting to hedge portfolios. Most market participants overlook the versatility and flexibility of options.

22. One of the put/call ratios more widely used by traders today is computed as the total volume of puts divided by the total volume of calls on the ___________.

    Answer: A—Chicago Board Options Exchange

    Discussion: The CBOE put-to-call ratio is one of the best gauges of market sentiment. It is computed as the total number of puts divided by the total number of calls traded each day on the Chicago Board Options Exchange. The ratio is also updated throughout the day and available on the Chicago Board Options Exchange web site (www.cboe.com).

23. When the CBOE put-to-call ratio rises toward the high end or above 1.00—as it did in the fall of 1998, right before the market hit bottom—traders should become alert for ___________.

Answer: B—Buying opportunities

Discussion: There is more call than put buying when dealing with stock options. For that reason, the total CBOE put/call ratio is generally less than 1.00. As a result, a reading of 1.00 or more from the CBOE put-to-call ratio is a sign of relatively high levels of put activity or bearish bets. In that situation, the contrary thinker will theoretically become more bullish and look for buying opportunities in the stock market.

24. When stocks fall, put buying ____________; when stocks leap forward, call activity ____________.

Answer: B—Rises/Increases

Discussion: Most option traders are trend followers and are attracted to moving prices. When stocks begin to slide, the reaction is to purchase puts. Conversely, during market rallies speculators try to profit through call buying.

25. True or False: When the CBOE put-to-call ratio rises toward the high end or above 1.00, it is a sign of excessive market pessimism and heavy put buying.

Answer: True

Discussion: The CBOE put-to-call ratio almost always remains between .50 and 1.00. It is computed as total put activity divided by total call activity on the Chicago Board Options Exchange. Since there is almost always more call activity than put activity, it remains below 1.00 the majority of the time. When investors become anxious and put activity increases, it will sometimes rise above 1.00. Such readings are rare, however, and generally signal excessive pessimism.

Media Assignment

Sentiment analysis is more art than science. There is no way to know with certitude if the trading crowd has become extremely bullish or bearish. Still, there are several tools that can help. The important thing to understand is that the market is like a manic-depressive beast. Emotions can drive it to extremes. When investors become euphoric, it is time to turn cautious. But when pessimism and bearishness prevail, the door is opened for a market rally. The crowd is generally on the wrong side of the market during important turning points. Sentiment indicators help quantify relative levels of optimism and pessimism and help pinpoint extremes. Importantly, the interpretation of the data will vary from one trader to the next.

The goal is to develop an arsenal of tools or gauges that can help identify extremes of emotion. Some are more subjective and involve the study of the headlines from the financial press and commentary from the market pundits or gurus. Others are more objective. The CBOE put-to-call ratio is an example of a gauge that is reliable because it reflects the actual trading decisions of option players, and not merely guesswork or hunches. It is worth monitoring on a daily basis. VIX, VXN, and QQV are implied volatility indicators that can be viewed with any quote service. Other sentiment indicators include surveys of newsletter writers, short interest ratios, levels of margin debt, and the market for initial public offerings. Space limits a full description of each, but they can easily be found in *Barron's*, the *Wall Street Journal*, and a column entitled "Sentiment Journal" posted weekly at Optionetics.com. Take the time to keep an eye on your choice of sentiment indicators. See how the changes in these indicators affect different stocks in various sectors as well as your paper trades. Find the places where trends and reversals correspond to sentiment extremes. Write it all down in your trading journal to help you remember what the market is telling you.

Vocabulary List

Contrarian: An investor who trades against the crowd. When the majority of investors are bullish, the contrarian will turn bearish. When pessimism or fear prevail, the contrary thinker will turn bullish. Contrary thinking can be applied to the entire market, a specific industry, or an individual stock.

DJX: The ticker symbol for the Dow Jones Industrial Average options that trade on the Chicago Board Options Exchange. DJX is an index equal to one-hundredth of the value of the Dow Jones Industrial Average.

Extremes: Periods of time when the mass of investors turns overly bullish or bearish. Extremes are caused primarily by two emotions: fear and greed. It generally pays to bet against the extremes.

Market bottom: When, after a prolonged period of falling prices, stocks stop falling. Market bottoms occur at the end of bear markets. Investors have generally turned bearish and sold off a large amount of their stock holdings.

Market top: When, after a prolonged period of rising prices, stocks no longer move higher. Market tops occur at the end of bull markets when investors have invested a significant amount of capital in the stock market and have become predominantly bullish.

MNX: The ticker symbol for the Mini-Nasdaq 100, which is an index equal to one-tenth the value of the Nasdaq 100 index (NDX).

Nasdaq 100 (NDX): An index consisting of 100 of the largest nonfinancial stocks trading on the Nasdaq Stock Market. Therefore, NDX includes mostly technology and biotechnology companies.

OEX: The ticker symbol for the S&P 100 Index, the first index to have listed options. The index consists of 100 of the largest stocks trading on the U.S. stock exchanges that also have options linked to their performance.

Put/call ratio: This indicator is simply the number of puts traded each day divided by call volume. It can be applied to an individual stock, an index, or by exchange. Put-to-call ratios give the trader a sense of whether traders are predominantly bullish or bearish.

QQQ: The Nasdaq 100 QQQ is an exchange-traded fund that is designed to equal one-fortieth of the Nasdaq 100 Index. Unlike indexes, the QQQ settles for shares and not cash. In addition, QQQ options settle American-style. The Nasdaq 100 QQQ was originally called the Nasdaq 100 Index Trust.

QQV: The QQQ Volatility Index (QQV) was launched on January 23, 2001. The index is designed to measure the implied volatility on the popular Nasdaq 100 QQQ options. Like VXN and VIX, QQV is an implied volatility index.

S&P 500 (SPX): An index consisting of 500 of the largest companies with shares listed for trading on the U.S. stock exchanges.

Sentiment analysis: The process of studying the psychology of the market. It is an ongoing effort in determining whether investors are primarily bullish or bearish. Sentiment analysis also involves the art of contrary thinking. That is, it requires the assumption that the general investment public is usually wrong at major turning points in the market. When the public, or the crowd as it is sometimes called, is optimistic or bullish on the market, the contrary thinker will take a negative or bearish stance toward the market. When the prevailing psychology is overly bearish or pessimistic toward the stock market, the contrarian will develop a more bullish stance toward stocks. The goal is to identify extremes of optimism or pessimism, and then bet in the opposite direction.

Speculative activity: Aggressive trading in search of quick short-term gains, often pursued by speculators hoping to profit from put and call buys. Therefore, high levels of options trading often indicate excessive speculative activity.

VIX: The CBOE Volatility Index, or VIX, is the market's "fear gauge." In addition, it is a measure of implied volatility on S&P 100 (OEX) options. During times of market turbulence, investors will turn to OEX put options for protection. The aggressive buying of OEX puts, in turn, often leads to a surge in implied volatility and a rise in VIX. Therefore, when VIX rises, it is a sign of investor angst; when VIX falls to low levels, it suggests investor bullishness or complacency.

VXN: The Nasdaq 100 Volatility Index, or VXN, was developed early in 2001 by the CBOE. It is similar to VIX, but measures the implied volatility on Nasdaq 100 index (NDX) options, instead of the OEX. The trader is looking for relatively low readings (45–50%) from VXN to presage a market top. High readings (75% and higher) signal extreme market fear and are a sign of a market bottom and that the market is set to rebound. Closing VIX and VXN readings are listed in Optionetics.com's weekly column, "Sentiment Journal," and traders can get intraday readings by typing in $VIX or $VXN in the quote box at the Optionetics.com home page.

8

Exploiting Low Volatility

Answers and Discussions

1. If implied volatility is high, an option appears ____________.

   Answer: B—Expensive

   Discussion: Implied volatility is one of the determinants of an option's price. It is always in a state of change. When it expands, it causes the option premium to rise. Therefore, when implied volatility is high, the options are considered expensive.

2. The more confused a market is, the better chance an option has of ending up ____________.

   Answer: A—In-the-money

   Discussion: If a stock has been trading within a large range, it suggests a fair amount of confusion. The stock can rise or fall significantly in value within a few days or a few weeks. As a result, the odds that the stock will reward call holders by rising above a given strike price, or profit put owners by dropping below a set strike price, are greater. In short, the odds of the stock making a significant move higher or lower are greater in a more confused market and, in that case, the options have a better chance of being in-the-money at expiration.

3. The maximum risk of buying a call is limited to the ____________.

   Answer: D—Call premium × 100

   Discussion: The maximum risk associated with owning a call is the amount invested when purchasing the call. The cost of the call, in turn, is equal to the option premium times the multiplier, which is 100.

4. The long call is ___________ when the price of the underlying asset rises above the strike price of the call.

   Answer: A—In-the-money

   Discussion: In-the-money (ITM) describes an option with intrinsic value. For a call, this means that the strike price is below the current market price for the stock, and that if the call is exercised the stock can be sold in the market at the current market price for a profit.

5. Fill in the blanks in the candlestick diagram in Figure 8.2 using the terms in the adjacent box (some words are used twice).

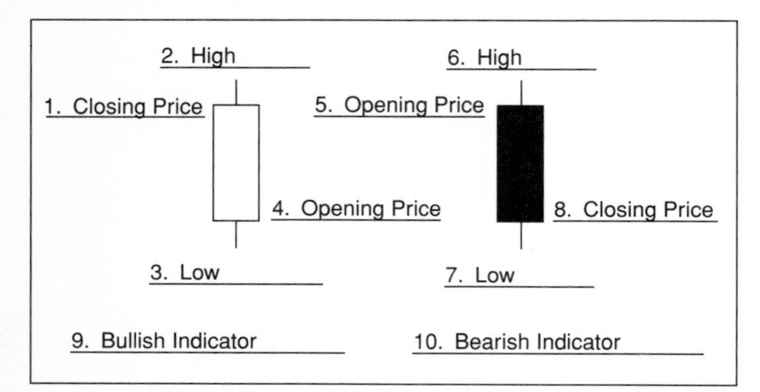

Opening Price
Closing Price
High
Low
Bearish Indicator
Bullish Indicator

Figure 8.2 Candlestick Diagram—Answer

6. A call's premium will ___________ in value depending on how high the underlying instrument ___________ in price beyond the strike price of the call.

   Answer: C—Increase/Rises

   Discussion: Call options represent the right, but not the obligation, to buy a stock at a specific price until expiration. Therefore, as the stock price moves higher, the call option, or right, takes on greater value. When the stock price rises above the strike price of the call, the option has intrinsic value. That is, it can be exercised and a profit can be captured (by purchasing the stock at the strike price and selling it in the market at a higher price). The further the stock price rises above the strike price, the greater the intrinsic value of the option.

7. A strategist will go long a put option in anticipation that the stock or index will ___________.

   Answer: B—Fall

   Discussion: Puts increase in value when the price of the underlying asset falls. Therefore, traders will often buy puts on a stock or an index when they expect it to fall.

8. True or False: The premium of a long put option will show up as a credit in your trading account.

   Answer: False

   Discussion: A long put is another way of saying a purchased put. (Short puts refer to the sale of puts.) Whether long puts or calls, the strategist is paying premiums in exchange for the rights granted by the options. Payments for premiums, in turn, are reflected as debits, not credits, in one's trading account.

9. True or False: A put option is in-the-money (ITM) when the strike price is higher than the market price of the underlying asset.

   Answer: True

   Discussion: Only an in-the-money option has intrinsic value. Intrinsic value arises when the price of the underlying asset falls below the strike price of the put or rises above the strike price of the call.

10. True or False: The bear put spread involves the simultaneous purchase of a put option and sale of a put option, with different expiration dates, but the same strike prices.

    Answer: False

    Discussion: The bear put spread involves the purchase and sale of two options with the same expiration date, but different strike prices. The trade involves the purchase of a higher strike put and the sale of a lower strike put.

11. When using the bull call spread, the strategist anticipates the stock or index to

    ____________.

    Answer: A—Rise

    Discussion: The bull call spread involves the purchase and sale of two calls with the same expiration months, but different strike prices. Using this strategy, the trader buys a lower strike call and sells a higher strike call. Profits arise when the stock price heads higher, with the maximum gain happening when the stock price rises above the higher of the two strike prices.

12. True or False: The bull call spread is more likely to feel a negative impact from falling IV than the bear put spread.

    Answer: True

    Discussion: The bull call spread is likely to be adversely affected by falling implied volatility because IV often falls when a stock or index moves higher. Therefore, although the strategist may be correct in implementing a bull call spread and watching the stock or index move higher, falling IV can have a negative impact on the overall position. Implied volatility, however, tends to rise as a stock or index falls. Therefore, the bear put spread, which profits when the underlying asset falls, is less likely to feel the negative impact of falling IV.

13. True or False: The call ratio backspread is a type of trade that is best used when implied volatility is low.

    Answer: True

    Discussion: Call ratio backspreads are strategies that work best in a low volatility environment. The strategy involves selling lower strike calls and buying a greater number of higher strike calls (the ratio must be less than $^2/_3$). Ideally, the trade is done for a credit; that is, the premium from selling the calls is greater than the premium paid for buying the calls. This is only possible when options are relatively cheap—when IV is low.

14. It is best to purchase straddles when implied volatility is ___________.

    Answer: B—Low

    Discussion: Straddles involve the simultaneous purchase of a put and a call on the same stock, with the same expiration dates and strike prices. Since the trade requires buying both a put and a call, it is best established when options are cheap (i.e., implied volatility is low). Buying a straddle when IV is high can lead to a loss due to a drop in the implied volatility—hence the value is sucked out of the option premiums as well.

15. True or False: Entry into either a call or put ratio backspread requires high levels of implied volatility.

    Answer: False

    Discussion: Ultimately, the ratio backspread is most attractive when it can be done for a credit. In that way, even if the stock does not move in the anticipated direction—higher for calls or lower for puts—the strategist keeps the credit from establishing the trade. High levels of implied volatility make ratio backspreads difficult because the option premiums will be higher and it will not be easy to establish the trade for a credit.

16. Calculate the maximum reward and risk, as well as breakevens, for the following trades with XYZ trading at 40:

    Long Call: Long 1 Oct XYZ 40 Call @ 3

    Strategy = Buy 1 call option

    Maximum Reward = Unlimited to the upside

    Maximum Risk = Limited to the call premium × 100 = 3 × 100 = $300

    Breakeven = Strike price + call premium = 40 + 3 = 43

    Long Put: Long 1 Oct XYZ 40 Put @ 2.50

    Strategy = Buy 1 put option

    Maximum Reward = Limited to the downside as the stock falls to zero

    Maximum Risk = Limited to the put premium × 100 = 2.50 × 100 = $250

    Breakeven = Strike price – put premium = 40 – 2.50 = 37.50

Long Straddle: Long 1 Oct XYZ 40 Call @ 3 and Long 1 Oct XYZ 40 Put @ 2.50

Strategy = Buy an ATM put and an ATM call with the same expiration

Maximum Reward = Unlimited above and below breakevens

Maximum Risk = Limited to the net debit of the options = (3 + 2.50) × 100 = $550

Upside Breakeven = Strike price + net debit = 40 + 5.50 = 45.50

Downside Breakeven = Strike price – net debit = 40 – 5.50 = 34.50

Bear Put Spread: Long 1 Oct XYZ 45 Put @ 4 and Short 1 Oct XYZ 35 Put @ 1.25

Strategy = Buy a higher strike put and sell a lower strike put with the same expiration

Maximum Reward = (Difference in strikes – net debit) × 100 = [(45 – 35) – 2.75] × 100 = $725

Maximum Risk = Limited to the net debit paid for the options = (4 – 1.25) × 100 = $275

Breakeven = Higher strike – net debit = 45 – 2.75 = 42.25

Bull Call Spread: Long 1 Oct XYZ 35 Call @ 5 and Short 1 Oct XYZ 45 Call @ 1.50

Strategy = Sell a higher strike call and buy a lower strike call with the same expiration

Maximum Reward = (Difference in strikes – net debit) × 100 = [(45 – 35) – 3.50] × 100 = $650

Maximum Risk = Limited to the net debit paid for the options = (5 – 1.50) × 100 = $350

Breakeven = Lower strike + net debit = 35 + 3.50 = 38.50

Call Ratio Backspread: Short 2 Oct XYZ 35 Calls @ 5 and Long 3 Oct XYZ 40 Calls @ 3

Strategy = Sell lower strike calls and buy a greater number of higher strike calls in a ratio of no more than $^2/_3$)

Net Credit = Short premiums – long premiums = [(2 × 5) – (3 × 3)] × 100 = $100

Maximum Reward = Unlimited to the upside beyond the breakeven. Limited to the net credit to the downside.

Maximum Risk = (# short calls × difference in strikes) × 100 – net credit = [2 × (40 – 35)] × 100 – 100 = $900

Upside Breakeven = Higher strike + [(difference in strikes × # short calls)/(# long calls – # short calls)] – net credit = 40 + [(40 – 35) × 2]/(3 – 2) – 1 = 49

Downside Breakeven = Lower strike + net credit = 35 + 1 = 36

Put Ratio Backspread: Short 2 Oct XYZ 40 Puts @ 2.50 and Long 3 XYZ 35 Puts @ 1.25

Strategy = Sell higher strike puts and buy a greater number of lower strike puts with a ratio no more than $^2/_3$

Net Credit = Short premiums – long premiums = [(2 × 2.5) – (3 × 1.25)] × 100 = $125

Maximum Reward = Limited to the downside as the underlying stock falls to zero. Limited to the net credit to the upside.

Maximum Risk = [(# short puts × difference in strikes) × 100] – net credit = [2 × (40 – 35)] × 100 – 125 = $875

Upside Breakeven = Higher strike – net credit = 40 – 1.25 = 38.75

Downside Breakeven = Lower strike – [(# short puts × difference in strikes)/(# long puts – # short puts)] + net credit = 35 – [2 × (40 – 35)/(3 – 2)] + 1.25 = 26.25

Media Assignment

Options trading can be among the most personally and financially rewarding experiences possible in life. The different trading scenarios and profit opportunities are too numerous to count. It is an ongoing challenge that pits the strategist against the marketplace. At the same time, however, many traders come away from the options market disappointed because consistently generating profits is not always easy. While it can be exciting and rewarding, disappointment often results from poorly timed directional bets. In addition, time decay and changes in implied volatility can also work against the options trader.

Unfortunately, no options book can teach you how to deal with the various adversities that options traders face. Only experience can. For that reason, the media assignments in this workbook focus on paper trading. Outside of actual trading, paper trading is the only way to develop a comprehensive understanding of how stock and option prices change through time and result in profits or losses.

Now, the reader should use the new material provided on the various strategies to establish a number of paper trades. In previous chapters, the covered call and the protective put were discussed. This section deals with low volatility strategies that arise when the strategist identifies cheap options—those with low levels of IV. The most basic low IV approach is the long put or the long call. While these benefit from increasing implied volatility, their success is more dependent on an eventual move higher (for calls) or lower (for puts). Therefore, the long call and long put are directional bets that can lead to significant losses if the stock moves in the wrong direction. Perhaps a better approach in a low volatility situation is a debit spread. A straddle can generate profits whether the stock moves higher or lower. However, since the straddle involves the purchase of both a put and a call, the strategy is best suited for a low implied volatility environment—when options are cheap. Similarly, when IV is low, the ratio backspread also provides attractive risk/reward potentials.

When a ratio backspread is established for a credit, the strategist can profit whether the stock moves higher or lower.

Most importantly, the trader wants to come away from this chapter with a few more arrows in the quiver. In this case, the arsenal includes trades that work best in a low implied volatility environment. Again, the assignment is to find a list of options that can be characterized as cheap. The easiest way to do so is with the free options ranker available on the Optionetics.com home page. Once the cheap options are found, the next step is to make an assessment of the possible future direction of the underlying asset. If the move is expected to be lower, paper trade bear put spreads and put ratio backspreads. If you expect the stock to move higher, plot out bull call spreads or call ratio backspreads. If the future direction is uncertain (but is expected to be explosive), create straddle trades on paper and add that important option strategy to your list of potential low implied volatility plays. Each strategy fits a specific market scenario. It's time to go hunting. Your job is to let each arrow find its prey by steadying your aim. Don't forget to find the fun in studying the markets. It's much easier to do something well if you fall in love with it.

Vocabulary List

Bear put spread: The simultaneous purchase and sale of two put options with the same expiration month, but different strike prices. The put with the higher strike price is bought, and a put with a lower strike price is sold. Bear put spreads yield limited profits when the underlying asset moves lower in price.

Bull call spread: The simultaneous purchase and sale of two call options with the same expiration month, but different strike prices. The call with the higher strike price is sold and a call with a lower strike price is purchased. Bull call spreads yield limited profits when the underlying asset moves higher in price.

Call ratio backspread: A call ratio backspread is constructed by purchasing calls with a higher strike price and selling fewer calls with a lower strike price at no cost or for a credit. The ratio of calls sold to those purchased is less than $^2/_3$; the most common ratios are 1:2 and 2:3. This means selling one call offset by buying two calls or selling two calls against buying three. The strategy is usually implemented at no cost, or sometimes for a net credit, because the premium received from selling the calls is often equal to, or greater than, the price paid for the long options.

Downside breakeven: The point at which a bearish trade has no profit or loss. It is the point at which the price of the underlying asset falls and the trader has recovered the cost of the trade.

Go long: To take on a position by purchasing a security. If an investor buys stock, he or she is going long the stock. Option traders go long puts or calls by purchasing the options as an opening transaction.

Go short: Selling an investment security. Selling a stock that is not already owned is an example of going short. Similarly, option traders selling either puts or calls have gone short.

Japanese candlestick: The method of technical analysis that was developed by the Japanese in the 1600s to study the price changes in rice contracts. It is a charting technique that is created from the same data used to create an ordinary price bar on a stock chart and displays the open, high, low, and closing prices of a stock or an index.

Long call: The purchase of call options as an opening transaction. Call holders, or owners, are said to be long calls.

Long put: The purchase of put options as an opening transaction. Therefore, the strategist who buys puts as a new position is said to be long puts.

Low volatility: A situation in which the premiums of an option contract have fallen due to a drop in the option's implied volatility.

Naked option: The opening sale of an option without owning the underlying security, or without any other hedge in the event of an adverse move in the underlying asset. For example, selling calls without owning the underlying stock is considered naked selling. If the naked call writer is assigned, he or she must purchase the stock at the current market price for delivery and is, therefore, caught naked.

Offset: To close an option position by either (1) selling an equal number of puts or calls with the same terms (expiration date and strike price) as the number of long put or call contracts held in the account, or (2) purchasing the same number of puts and calls with the same terms that are short within a trading account.

Options chain: A list of option prices sorted first by expiration month and then by strike price. Options chains are created as tables with calls on one half of the table and puts on the other half. Options chains generally include the last price, the bid, the ask, trading volume, and open interest for each option contract.

Put ratio backspread: A put ratio backspread is constructed by purchasing puts and selling fewer puts with a higher strike price for no cost or at a credit. The ratio of puts sold to those purchased is generally less than $2/3$; the most common ratios are 1:2 and 2:3. This means selling one put offset by buying two puts or selling two puts against buying three. The strategy is usually implemented at no cost, or sometimes for a credit, because the premium received from selling the puts is often equal to, or greater than, the price paid for the long options.

Risk graph: A graphical view of the potential risk and rewards associated with an options trading position. The horizontal axis represents the underlying stock price, and the vertical axis represents the potential profit or loss of the trade.

Short call: The sale of a call option as an opening transaction. For example, covered calls involve being long stock and short calls.

Short put: The sale of a put option as an opening transaction. We do not recommend trading naked options.

Straddle: An options strategy that involves the simultaneous purchase of a put and a call with the same expiration month and strike price on the same underlying asset. Straddles are usually purchased using at-the-money options in anticipation that the underlying security will make a significant move higher or lower.

It is used when the future direction of the underlying asset is unknown, but expected to be large.

Upside breakeven: The point at which a bullish trade has no profit or loss. It is the point at which the price of the underlying asset rises and the trader can close the position and recover the cost of the trade.

Vega: The amount by which the value of an option changes for each percentage point change in implied volatility. For example, a stock option with a vega of .10 can be expected to increase 10 cents for every 1% increase in implied volatility.

9

Exploiting High Volatility

Answers and Discussions

1. True or False: Markets trading at a very low level of volatility have a high probability of a large move occurring.

   Answer: False

   Discussion: When a market is exhibiting low volatility, it is moving gradually higher, moderately lower, or simply sideways. It is not likely that, in such an environment, the market will make a large move.

2. True or False: When volatility is at a very high level, a substantial probability exists for the contract to maintain a trading range.

   Answer: False

   Discussion: High volatility means confusion in the marketplace and large fluctuations in prices. In that case, the option contracts are not likely to remain range bound—they're likely to make significant price moves higher or lower instead.

3. VIX is a sentiment analysis indicator that measures ____________.

   Answer: C—Crowd psychology

   Discussion: VIX is a measure of crowd psychology. It is a measure of the level of volatility currently priced into the S&P 100 index options. Therefore, VIX tends to rise when investors expect greater volatility going forward. Investors generally expect volatility to increase when there is a fair amount of uncertainty, anxiety, or fear in the marketplace. In sum, high VIX means fear in the market is high, and, therefore, it is a measure of crowd psychology. In fact, it is sometimes called the "fear gauge."

4. True or False: When the VIX is high, it's time to buy volatility; when the VIX is low, it's time to sell volatility.

   Answer: False

   Discussion: The adage, "when VIX is high, it's time to buy" does not refer to buying volatility. Instead, when VIX is high, investors are better off buying stocks because the market has probably been driven down by fear; therefore, prices are low and probably will bounce back.

5. The ____________ is a popular option strategy in which one call is sold to create an open short position against 100 shares of stock already owned by the option seller.

   Answer: D—Covered call

   Discussion: The covered call is a simple stock option strategy that can be used to create income through the sale of call options. For every 100 shares of stock owned, one call contract is sold (as an opening transaction). The premium from the sale is then credited to the account. However, if the stock price rises above the strike price before expiration, the stock will probably be called away (and must be sold at the strike price of the option). Therefore, in exchange for the premium from the call, the investor gives up any potential profit opportunities should the stock rise significantly.

6. A ____________ is a put option where the writer of the contract does not have a short position in the underlying stock to cover the contract.

   Answer: E—Naked put option

   Discussion: The naked put is the sale of a put option without any other securities in the account to offset the risk of the position. Naked put options can result in significant losses should the stock price fall precipitously; if the options are exercised, the seller might be forced to buy the stock at a price (strike price) much higher than the current market price.

7. Whether selling naked puts or naked calls, the maximum profit is equal to the ____________.

   Answer: E—Premium received from the sale of the option

   Discussion: The reward from put selling is limited to the amount received from selling the put option. If the put is assigned, however, the seller will then be assigned the stock. Then, the loss becomes equal to the drop in the stock price minus the strike price of the option plus the premium received.

8. If you sell a naked put option, make sure it has less than ____________ days to expiration.

   Answer: B—30

   Discussion: Time decay is not linear and increases as expiration approaches. Therefore, options lose the most value in the 30 days prior to expiration. As an option seller, you want time decay working for you and, for that reason, it is better to sell short-term options with less than 45 days to expiration.

9. A deposit made by a trader with a clearinghouse to ensure that he or she will fulfill any financial obligations resulting from his or her trades is called ____________.

   Answer: C—Margin

   Discussion: Brokers will lend investors money to buy and sell investment securities, but they must maintain a minimum amount of equity (with cash, stocks, or other marginable securities) in order to borrow the trading funds. The amount of equity that is required within the account is called margin.

10. A broker's demand that a customer deposit additional funds to cover the price change of the underlying market in a trade is called a ____________.

    Answer: D—Margin call

    Discussion: If an investor's account drops below the minimum equity requirements of the brokerage firm, he or she is asked to either add more funds to the account or liquidate some of the positions. A margin call often results when the value of stock holdings falls significantly.

11. The two types of credit spreads are ____________.

    Answer: B—The bull put spread and the bear call spread

    Discussion: Credit spreads can be created with puts or calls. When using calls, the trade involves buying a higher strike call and selling a lower strike call. Since the call with the lower strike price will have a greater premium, the trade is established for a credit. In addition, profits arise when the stock price falls and both calls expire worthless. Therefore, it is a bearish trade involving calls—hence the name bear call spread. Credit spreads using puts, on the other hand, generally involve buying a lower strike put and selling a higher strike put. Profits are maximized when the stock price rises above both strike prices and the puts expire worthless. Therefore, using puts as part of a credit spread is often a bullish strategy—hence the name bull put spread.

12. True or False: A bull put spread involves selling a put with the strike price that is closest to the market value of the underlying asset (stock) and buying a lower strike put to hedge against unlimited risk.

    Answer: True

    Discussion: The bull put spread is similar to the naked put, but there is an important difference: The strategist is buying a put with a lower strike price to protect the position in the event of a sharp move lower in the stock. The premium received from the sale will be offset by the premium paid for the put with the lower strike price. However, in the event of a sharp move lower in the stock, the losses will be limited as well.

13. True or False: If you are selling high probability at-the-money or out-of-the-money put spreads, you will want to keep the time to expiration as long as possible.

    Answer: False

    Discussion: When selling options, the strategist is trying to benefit from the impact of time decay, which is not linear and increases as expiration approaches. Therefore, it is better to continually sell shorter-term options than attempt to sell options with more time until expiration.

14. A bear call spread is created by ____________ a call with a higher strike price and ____________ a call with a lower strike price.

    Answer: B—Purchasing/Selling

    Discussion: When using calls to establish a bearish credit spread, the trade involves buying a higher strike call and selling a lower strike call. Since the call with the lower strike price will have a greater premium (it has a greater chance of being in-the-money at expiration), the trade is established for a credit. In addition, profits arise when the stock price falls. It is therefore called a bearish spread.

15. True or False: In a forward volatility skew market, higher strike options have higher implied volatility and can be overpriced.

    Answer: True

    Discussion: The forward volatility skew is a situation where two options on the same stock, but with different strike prices, have different levels of implied volatility. The options with the higher strike price have higher implied volatility. The lower strike options have lower implied volatility. A large difference between the IV of the options can be a sign that the options with the higher strike price are overvalued. In that case, it makes sense to sell them. The following strategies work well in markets with forward volatility skews: bear put spreads, bull call spreads, and put ratio backspreads.

16. A reverse volatility skew is an excellent market scenario for which strategies?

    Answers: A—Bull put spread
    B—Bear call spread
    C—Call ratio backspread

    Discussion: A reverse volatility skew occurs when the lower strike options (the ones you want to sell) have higher implied volatility and can be overpriced. The higher strike options (the ones you want to buy) enjoy lower implied volatility and are often underpriced. In each of these strategies—bull put spreads, bear call spreads, and call ratio backspreads—you are selling lower strike options and buying higher strike options. Using markets with a reverse volatility skew should help to increase the potential profitability of the trade.

17. The butterfly spread is a market neutral trade that can use ____________.

    Answer: C—All calls or all puts

    Discussion: The butterfly can be created using all puts or all calls. Traders can vary the risk/reward potentials of the trade by using puts or calls. In all cases, however, the strategist is expecting the stock to stay within a range and for IV to fall.

18. True or False: If a combination of both calls and puts is created, it is called a golden butterfly.

    Answer: False

    Discussion: When the butterfly is created using both puts and calls, it is known as the iron butterfly—not the golden butterfly. An iron butterfly is a limited risk/limited reward high volatility strategy that combines both puts and calls. In contrast, a butterfly using only calls is generally referred to as a call butterfly; one with only puts is a put butterfly. The important factor to consider when creating butterflies is the implied volatility of the options; make sure to sell the options with the highest implied volatility and buy those with the lowest IV. That, in turn, will dictate whether to use an iron, put, or call butterfly strategy.

19. True or False: There are no strategies that can make money from a drop in volatility.

    Answer: False

    Discussion: There are a wide variety of options strategies that can profit regardless of changes in implied volatility. When IV is high and is expected to fall, the best strategies involve the net selling of options. Credit spreads, the covered call, and the butterfly are examples of strategies that work better in high IV situations.

20. Calculate the maximum reward and risk, as well as breakevens, for the following trades with XYZ trading at 50:

    Covered Call: Long 100 shares XYZ @ 50 and Short 1 Aug XYZ 55 Call @ 2.50

    Strategy = Buy the underlying security and sell an OTM call option

    Maximum Reward = Call premium + (strike price – initial stock price) × 100 = 2.50 + (55 – 50) × 100 = $750

    Maximum Risk = Limited to the downside below the breakeven as the underlying stock falls to zero

    Breakeven = Initial stock price – call premium = 50 – 2.50 = 47.50

    Short Put: Short 1 Aug XYZ 50 Put @ 4

    Strategy = Sell a put option

    Maximum Reward = Limited to the credit received from the put premium = 4 × 100 = $400

Maximum Risk = Limited as the stock price falls below the breakeven all the way to zero

Breakeven = Strike price – put premium = 50 – 4 = 46

Bull Put Spread: Long 1 Sept XYZ 45 Put @ 2 and Short 1 Sept XYZ 50 Put @ 4

Strategy = Buy a lower strike put and sell a higher strike put with the same expiration date

Maximum Reward = Limited to the net credit received = (4 – 2) × 100 = $200

Maximum Risk = Limited [(difference in strikes × 100) – net credit] = [(50 – 45) × 100] – 200 = $300

Breakeven = Higher strike – net credit = 50 – 2 = 48

Bear Call Spread: Long 1 Sept XYZ 55 Call @ 2.50 and Short 1 Sept XYZ 50 Call @ 5

Strategy = Buy a higher strike call and sell a lower strike call with the same expiration date

Maximum Reward = Limited to the net credit received = (5 – 2.50) × 100 = $250

Maximum Risk = Limited [(difference in strikes × 100) – net credit] = [(55 – 50) × 100 – 250 = $250

Breakeven = Lower strike + net credit = 50 + 2.50 = 52.50

Iron Butterfly Spread: Long 1 Sept XYZ 55 Call @ 2.50, Short 1 Sept XYZ 50 Call @ 5, Short 1 Sept XYZ 45 Put @ 2, Long 1 Sept XYZ 40 Put @ 1

Strategy = Buy a higher strike call at resistance, sell an ATM strike call, sell a lower strike put, and buy an even lower strike put at support

Maximum Reward = Limited to the net credit received = [(5 + 2) – (2.5 + 1)] × 100 = $350

Maximum Risk = Limited [(# of lowest strike options × difference between strikes) × 100] – net credit = [(1 × 5) × 100] – 350 = $150

Upside Breakeven = Strike price of short call + (net credit received = 50 + 3.50 = 53.50

Downside Breakeven = Strike price of short put – (net credit received = 45 – 3.50 = 41.50

Call Butterfly Spread: Long 1 Oct XYZ 45 Call @ 7, Short 2 Oct XYZ 55 Calls @ 5, Long 1 Oct XYZ 65 Call @ 1

Strategy = Buy lower strike call at support, sell two higher strike calls at equilibrium, and buy an even higher strike call at resistance

Maximum Reward: = Limited [(# of lowest strike options × difference in strikes) × 100] – net debit = [(1 × 10) × 100] – 200 = $800

Maximum Risk = Limited to the net debit paid = [(2 × 5) – (7 + 1)] × 100 = $200

Upside Breakeven = Highest strike price – net debit = 65 – 2 = 63

Downside Breakeven = Lowest strike price + (net debit/# of lowest strikes) = 45 + 2 = 47

Put Butterfly Spread: Long 1 Sept XYZ 40 Put @ 1, Short 2 Sept XYZ 50 Puts @ 4, Long 1 Sept XYZ 60 Put @ 6

Strategy = Buy lower strike put, sell two higher strike puts, and buy an even higher strike put

Maximum Reward = Limited [(# of lowest strike options × difference in strikes) × 100] – net debit = [(1 × 10) × 100] – 100 = $900

Maximum Risk = Limited to the net debit = [(2 × 4) – (1 + 6)] × 100 = $100

Upside Breakeven = Highest strike price – net debit = 60 – 1 = 59

Downside Breakeven = Lowest strike price + (net debit/# of lowest strikes) = 40 + 1 = 41

Media Assignment

There are several different strategies that can make money when implied volatility falls. Some, such as short calls and puts, have higher risks than do others such as credit spreads and butterflies. There is rarely one strategy that is right for everyone. The ones discussed in this chapter are among the most popular, and relatively easy to understand. The important factor to consider is that when you apply these strategies to high volatility markets, you can expect to get a better risk/reward situation than you would implementing these strategies in a low volatility situation. Remember, it is better to be an insurance salesperson when everyone needs insurance the most than when no one needs insurance; the premiums are greater and the ability to keep some or all of the premiums is greater, too. In a high volatility environment, the strategist wants to think like the insurance salesperson.

Paper trading is truly the best way to start learning how to trade high volatility option strategies. Doing so will also help you find the specific trades that work best for you. In fact, high volatility might not be a strategy that fits your investment style. Or you might find that you like these strategies best and end up trading nothing but high IV markets. There is nothing wrong with either approach. You are encouraged to learn a large number of strategies and then focus on the few that seem to fit your investment style best. Paper trading rather than actually implementing new strategies is sometimes a great way to find out that the strategy in question doesn't fit your investment style. Check out the paper trading templates in the Appendix.

Vocabulary Definitions

Bear call spread: Buying a higher strike call and simultaneously selling a call with a lower strike price. Since the call with the lower strike price will have a higher premium, the trade is established for a credit. In addition, profits arise when the stock price falls. It is therefore called a bear call spread.

Bull put spread: Buying a lower strike put and selling a put with a higher strike price. Profits are maximized when the stock price rises above both strike prices and the puts expire worthless. Therefore, using puts as part of a credit spread is often a bullish strategy—hence the name bull put spread. In addition, since the put with the lower strike price will command a higher price, the trade is established as a credit.

Call butterfly spread: A butterfly spread that involves only calls. In this case, the strategist buys a lower strike option at support, sells two higher strike options at equilibrium, and buys an even higher strike option at resistance (all calls). The trader expects range bound trading and a drop in IV. Also known as a long butterfly spread.

Covered call: The covered call involves the sale of calls against stock that is already owned. The purchase of the stock and the sale of the call can take place simultaneously, or the calls can be sold against stock that is already held in a portfolio. For investors, the covered call is considered a way of generating additional income from a stock holding. It is also considered less risky than simply owning the stock because the premium earned from selling the call offsets some of the cost of the stock. However, it is not a risk-free trade, and losses can result if the stock falls below the downside breakeven.

Credit spread: A strategy that yields a credit in a trader's account. A bull put spread, which involves the purchase of a lower strike put and the sale of a higher strike put, is an example of a credit spread. Bear call spreads are another. Sometimes ratio backspreads can also be established for a credit. Basically, any trade where the premium received from selling options is greater than the premium paid for purchasing options is considered a credit spread.

Forward volatility skew: A volatility price skew where higher strike options have higher implied volatility than options with lower strike prices (on the same stock with the same expiration date).

Iron butterfly spread: An option trade that involves both puts and calls. In this case, the strategist buys a higher strike call at resistance, sells an ATM strike call, sells a lower strike put, and buys an even lower strike put at support. The iron butterfly works best when the strategist expects range bound trading and a drop in implied volatility.

Margin: A deposit made by a trader with a clearinghouse to ensure that he or she will fulfill any financial obligations resulting from his or her trades. This amount will change as the price of the investment changes.

Margin call: A broker's demand that a customer deposit additional funds to cover the price change of the underlying market in a trade. Margin calls usually occur after a stock holding has fallen in value. The deposit must be made immediately or the broker will be forced to close the position, often at a loss to the trader.

Naked put: Selling a put without any offsetting positions in other puts, calls, or the underlying stock. Naked put selling is an aggressive strategy that can lead to substantial losses in the event that the stock falls. However, some investors use the strategy as a way to buy a stock. That is, instead of buying the stock, the investor sells the put. If the stock falls below the strike price of the put, chances are the investor will be assigned (put) the stock and, therefore, will then own the stock at a higher price than it is currently worth.

Put butterfly spread: This trade involves only puts. In this strategy, the trader buys a lower strike option at support, sells two higher strike options at equilibrium, and buys an even higher strike option (all puts) at resistance. Also known as a long butterfly spread.

Reverse volatility skew: A volatility price skew where the lower strike options have higher implied volatility than the higher strike options (on the same stock with the same expiration).

10

Volatility Skews

Answers and Discussions

1. True or False: A volatility skew is created when two or more options on the same underlying stock or index have no difference in terms of implied volatility.

   Answer: False

   Discussion: Volatility skews exist when two or more options on the same underlying stock have *different* levels of implied volatility. There are two types of volatility skews to look for: volatility price skews and volatility time skews. Price skews exist when the implied volatility differs across strike prices of options on the same stock and the same expiration months. Time skews are identified by different levels of implied volatility on stock options with the same strike prices, but different expiration months.

2. True or False: On the volatility smile skew graph, the higher the volatility, the steeper the skew is likely to be.

   Answer: True

   Discussion: A skew graph that shows a smile has deep in-the-money (ITM) and deep out-of-the-money (OTM) options with high IV. That is, a volatility smile represents options that are above and below the at-the-money option demonstrating high volatility. The higher the volatility of the OTM and ITM options, the bigger the smile.

3. A volatility frown skew graph represents low IV options that are __________ the at-the-money strike price.

   Answer: E—Above and below

Discussion: A volatility frown is the opposite of the smile. In this case, the OTM and ITM options have lower volatility than the at-the-money options. When the graph is plotted, it takes on the shape of an upside-down U, or a frown.

4. True or False: The volatility frown is the most common skew graph.

   Answer: False

   Discussion: Not the frown, but the volatility smile is the most popular of skew graphs and appears the most often.

5. The volatility slope skew graph goes in ____________ direction(s).

   Answer: B—One

   Discussion: Unlike the smile, which is shaped like a U, or the frown, which appears as an upside-down U, the volatility slope shows volatility increasing in one direction—either toward the out-of-the-money options or toward the in-the-money options.

6. True or False: The best way to take advantage of skew is to remember the simple rule: Buy high (implied volatility) and sell low (implied volatility).

   Answer: False

   Discussion: Buying low (implied volatility) and selling high (implied volatility) is one of the most important rules for the volatility trader to follow. Low IV leads to lower-priced options while high IV leads to higher-priced options. To enhance your success, always buy low and sell high.

7. True or False: Volatility skews between months happen when the options with the same strike price but different expiration months have different levels of implied volatility.

   Answer: True

   Discussion: Also known as volatility time skews, these exist when there are different levels of implied volatility on options on the same underlying asset with the same strike prices but different expiration months. Time skews can create trading opportunities. For instance, if the short-term options (with one or two months left until expiration) have much higher levels of implied volatility than long-term options (with the most time until expiration), the higher IV will make the short-term contract more expensive compared to the long-term contract. In that case, the strategist can consider buying the long-term contract and selling the short-term contract. The strategy is known as a calendar spread and is one of the most popular ways of taking advantage of time skews.

8. A horizontal spread involves the purchase of a ____________ and the sale of a ____________ with the same strike price.

   Answer: A—Longer-term call/Shorter-term call

Discussion: Also known as the calendar spread, the horizontal spread takes advantage of time skews. In general, the horizontal spread is established by selling a short-term option (put or call) with high IV and buying a longer-term option (put or call) with lower implied volatility.

9. True or False: Diagonal spreads involve different strike prices.

   Answer: True

   Discussion: Diagonal spreads can be created in a number of ways using either all puts or all calls. In each instance, however, when establishing a diagonal spread the strike prices and expiration months are different. For example, if the strategist is bullish on a stock trading at $50 a share and expects a gradual move higher, he or she can purchase the long-term call with a strike price of 60 and offset it with the sale of a short-term call with a strike price of 55. The idea is that the stock will make a gradual move higher, but the short-term option (with a strike price of 55) will expire worthless. Then, the long-term call can be held in anticipation of a move above 60 after the short-term call expires. In this case, it is a diagonal spread because both the strike prices and expiration months are different.

10. Diagonal spreads using calls can be created if there is a volatility skew between the ____________ and the strategist is ____________ on the stock.

    Answer: B—Short-term and long-term options/Bearish

    Discussion: Diagonal spreads can be created in a number of ways. One way is to create a spread when there is a skew between the short-term call (with a lower strike price) and the long-term call (with a higher strike price). The trade is done for a credit. If the strategist is bearish, this makes sense because the short-term option will lose value faster than the long-term option. If the stock falls below the strike price of the short call, the trader keeps the credit. If not, there is protection against an upside move in the stock from the long-term call.

11. The primary objective of the calendar spread is to have time eat away at the ____________ option while the ____________ option retains its value.

    Answer: D—Short/Long

    Discussion: Time decay does not happen in a linear manner. Instead, short-term options will experience greater time value loss because the rate of decay increases as expiration approaches. This can work to the trader's advantage. Specifically, the calendar spread sells the option with the faster rate of time decay (the short-term option) and buys the option with the slower rate of time decay (the longer-term option).

12. The maximum risk of a calendar spread is equal to ____________.

    Answer: D—Long premium minus short premium

    Discussion: The calendar spread involves the purchase and sale of two options with the same strike price but different expiration dates. Therefore, the long option provides protection in case the short option is assigned. In other words, if the strategist expects assignment, he or she can close the position or exercise the long option upon assignment. Either way, the maximum risk to the trade is the difference between the long and short premiums.

13. A calendar spread can lose money if ___________.

    Answer: C—The stock price moves too high before the short call expires

    Discussion: Calendar spreads are suitable for a market that is moving gradually in one direction or the other. Sharp moves higher will lead to assignment on the short option for a call calendar spread, and quick moves lower work against the short-term option in a put calendar spread.

14. True or False: The put calendar spread is appealing if expectations are that the stock will rise.

    Answer: False

    Discussion: The put calendar spread is a neutral or bearish strategy. It is suitable when the strategist expects the stock to move sideways or gradually lower.

15. Name the two keys to creating successful calendar spreads.

    Answers:

    1. Map out each trade in terms of risk/reward potential and plot them on a risk graph.
    2. Identify attractive volatility skews between the front month and back month options.

    Discussion:

    1. Mapping out the risk/reward potential is important for any options trade, including calendar spreads. Doing so provides the strategist a way to gauge whether the trade has appeal. In addition, the risk graph can help the strategist establish an exit strategy by identifying the point at which the trade begins to incur losses.
    2. The key to identifying attractive calendar spreads is to find a situation where the short-term options are more expensive than the long-term options. This is of paramount importance to the volatility trader—buying low and selling high implied volatility IV.

16. The types of volatility skews that can be useful in finding trading opportunities are ___________.

    Answer: D—A and B (volatility price skews and volatility time skews)

    Discussion: Both price skews and time skews can be useful in identifying trading opportunities. Price skews exist when the implied volatility differs across strike prices of options on the same stock and the same expiration months. Time skews are identified by different levels of implied volatility on stock options with the same strike prices but different expiration months.

17. True or False: The strike prices for a set of options cannot have different levels of implied volatility.

    Answer: False

    Discussion: Price skews result from different levels of implied volatility on a set of options on the same underlying asset with the same expiration months, but different strike prices. It is not uncommon to see price skews—especially in the index market.

18. When trading resumed following the terrorist attacks of September 11, 2001, volatility ____________.

    Answer: C—Rose

    Discussion: After the market closure following the terrorist attacks on September 11, 2001, trading resumed on September 17. At that time, there was a lot of pent-up selling (and a little buying). As a result, trading volume surged when the market resumed and volatility became quite high.

19. True or False: Demand will never cause a volatility skew.

    Answer: False

    Discussion: Heavy demand will often cause a volatility skew. For example, when traders expect an aggressive short-term move higher in a stock (for instance, in the case of a takeover rumor), the front-month or near-term options will often see a jump in demand. As a result, the short-term options will have much higher IV, and a time skew will result. This is a good environment for placing calendar spreads.

20. Philip Morris is often considered a defensive stock because ____________.

    Answer: B—It generally performs well when most stocks head lower.

    Discussion: Defensive stocks perform well when the broader market moves lower. Generally, defensive stocks have stable earnings and are not sensitive to changes in the economy. Tobacco, food, and utility stocks are examples of defensive stocks. Philip Morris is both a tobacco and a food company.

Media Assignment

Perhaps there are a few get-rich-quick schemes that work; unfortunately, not many people have stumbled across any. Trading options is definitely *not* one of them. Trading options successfully takes a fair amount of intelligence, persistence, knowledge, and experience. Anyone can achieve significant financial rewards in the options market, but it is not always an easy proposition. Ultimately, you will find the strategies that work for you. Perhaps a winning strategy will be in the index market, or trading the Qs. Maybe you have a knack for identifying reversal candidates and placing directional trades. Or perhaps nondirectional trades such as straddles and ratio backspreads will hold the ticket to your success.

If you have followed the suggestions from the media assignments in this book, you have created a journal that includes a number of paper trades and a host of different strategies. Each is designed to provide a trading plan for a particular market environment. If implied volatility is low, debit spreads, long calls or puts, backspreads, and straddles work best. If volatility is high, the trader should consider credit spreads, butterflies, or covered calls. When the strategist sees large volatility time skews between options on the same contract, horizontal or diagonal spreads can offer attractive risk/reward potentials. By now the paper trading journal should have examples of each of these trades—along with quotes for the entry price, time frames and price targets, exit prices, and profits/losses. The importance of trading on paper before risking actual trading capital can't be overemphasized.

At some point, however, there is no substitute for real-world experience. The first step in attaining that hands-on experience is to identify a broker, which is the final media assignment in this workbook. The importance of finding a reliable broker cannot be overlooked. For those with relatively little trading experience, a significant amount of research is necessary. However, in today's market the list of brokers can be narrowed down to those with online trading capabilities, and the book *Trade Options Online* is a fine starting point. In addition, there is a broker review section at Optionetics.com that provides most of the necessary details regarding the chief brokerage firms with options-related services. Finally, the message boards at Optionetics.com include a broker section where experienced and novice traders meet to share ideas about brokerage firms. On those same boards, there is also a forum under my name, Tom Gentile. Feel free to drop by and send me a message or options-related question anytime.

Vocabulary Definitions

Back month: The option contract in a series that is the last to expire. In other words, the options with the longest time until expiration.

Calendar spread: A spread that consists of buying and selling options (all puts or all calls) on the same stock with the same strike prices, but with different expiration dates. It involves selling an ATM short-term option and buying an ATM long-term option on the same underlying stock with the same strike price. The trade can be established with either puts or calls. The idea is for time decay (which impacts short-term options to a greater degree than long-term options) to eat away at the option that has been sold. The longer-term option will hold more value because time decay is greater as expiration approaches. For instance, the strategist who believes a $50 stock will move sideways or gradually higher, can purchase the January 2003 55 call and simultaneously sell the October 2002 55 call. The goal is to see the short-term option expire worthless and then for the stock to move above 55 to make the long-term call profitable. After the short-term call expires worthless, the strategist can also opt to sell another short-term call against the long call. A market with a volatility time skew is best used when placing a calendar spread because you are selling a short-term option and buying a long-term option. The idea is to buy low implied volatility and sell high implied volatility.

Defensive stock: A stock that performs well when the general market moves lower. Generally, defensive stocks have stable earnings and are not sensitive to changes in the economy. Tobacco, food, and utility stocks are examples of defensive stocks.

Diagonal spread: Diagonal spreads can be created in a number of ways using either all puts or all calls. In each instance, however, the strike prices and expiration months are different. Using all puts or all calls, diagonal spreads combine different strike prices and expiration months. For instance, if a strategist is bearish on the S&P 100 (OEX) with a current price of 450 and expects a gradual move lower, a long-term put for 425 can be purchased and a shorter-term put with a strike price of 435 can be sold. The sale of the short-term put partially offsets the purchase of the longer-term put. In this case, the strategist wants the short-term put to expire worthless and then hold the long-term put after the short-term put expires in anticipation of a move lower. After the short-term option expires, the strategist can also opt to sell another short-term option. Diagonal spreads can be created using puts or calls and structured whether the strategist is bullish or bearish on the underlying asset. Since you are selling different expiration months and strike prices, diagonal spreads are best employed when a market is exhibiting either price or time skews.

Front month: The option contract in a series that is nearest to expiration. On January 1, the front month contract would be the January options, because they expire on the third Saturday of that month. That is, they are the next to expire.

Frown: An upside-down U-shaped skew graph that shows the out-of-the-money and in-the-money options with low levels of implied volatility compared to the at-the-money options.

Horizontal spread: A spread that consists of buying and selling options (all puts or all calls) on the same stock with the same ATM strike prices, but with different expiration dates. Also known as a calendar spread.

Liquidity: (1) The amount of cash within an account, economy, or portfolio. The more cash, the greater the liquidity. (2) The ability to quickly convert an investment to cash. Stocks and options are generally considered liquid investments because they can easily be converted to cash. (3) The amount of trading associated with a given investment security. The greater the trading volume of a stock or option, the greater its liquidity.

Options chain: A table including all of the strike price and expiration dates for a series of options. Chains generally include the option symbol, last trade, bid price, asking price, volume, and open interest.

Slope: A volatility skew graph that shows a gradual increase in implied volatility increasing in one direction.

Smile: A U-shaped skew graph that shows deep in-the-money (ITM) and deep out-of-the-money (OTM) options with high IV. A volatility smile represents options that have strike prices above and below the at-the-money option demonstrating high volatility. The higher the volatility of the OTM and ITM options, the bigger the smile.

Volatility price skew: When the implied volatility varies across a set of options on the same underlying asset with the same expiration months, but different strike prices.

Volatility time skew: When there are different levels of implied volatility on options on the same underlying asset with the same strike prices, but different expiration months.

Appendix
Paper Trading Templates

Long Call
Long Put
Protective Put
Covered Call
Bull Call Spread
Bear Put Spread
Bull Put Spread
Bear Call Spread
Call Ratio Backspread
Put Ratio Backspread
Long Straddle
Long Butterfly Spread
Long Iron Butterfly Spread
Calendar Spread
Diagonal Spread

Paper Trading Your Way to Success

Perhaps the best way to get the hang of trading options is to practice employing managed-risk options strategies through paper trading. The art of paper trading involves using real-time quotes and markets in hypothetical trades to test your knowledge and market savvy. The following pages are designed to help you apply the various options strategies reviewed in this book to real-world trading. The examples and templates in this section (Tables A.1 to A.30) provide an organized format for making calculations of a specific trade using an options strategy described in this manual as well as a way to track the progress of the trade. Feel free to photocopy the paper trading templates contained in this appendix as needed for additional practice. You should continue paper trading until you gain enough confidence in the use of each strategy to commit real money once a promising opportunity has been located.

For most investors, your paper trading prices will be based on those found on the Internet or in the *Wall Street Journal* or *Investor's Business Daily*. We highly recommend using Optionetics.com to get your quotes since we can attest to their accuracy. Once you have determined where to get the price quotes, you need to decide which stocks to use for each trade. Go back over the material in each chapter to determine what kind of market conditions need to appear in order to prompt the use of the right strategy. When you find a stock that looks appropriate, look up the list of available options and try out various combinations of strikes and months until you find the best trade you can using the calculations for maximum risk, maximum reward, and breakevens. Make sure to keep detailed notes as to why you chose that stock and any events that occur while you are waiting for the trade to become profitable on paper.

Once you decide on a trade, you can use the paper trading forms to track the progress of the trade as the prices fluctuate each day. You can also track it simultaneously using the portfolio service at Optionetics.com. Before you place the trade, make sure to decide on an exit price in case the trade loses money, and stick to it. Deciding ahead of time exactly how much money you can afford to lose is essential to becoming a successful options trader. Now, since you are simply paper trading, you may want to highlight your exit point and then continue to track the trade to see how it fares after this point. Although there will be times when your trade will turn around and head back into the profit zone, more often than not you'll get to witness it fall even further. But paper trading is about learning from your mistakes as much as it is learning from your successes, so get ready for an interesting journey. Do not expect the first few trades to make you a millionaire. Trading is a cumulative process that requires knowledge, experience, insight, and perseverance to master. Paper trading is a practical method of gaining experience without putting money on the line. Nonetheless, you must take this process seriously in order to learn. If you are diligent in your tracking process, you will gain a deeper understanding of each strategy that will serve you well when you enter the real-world marketplace.

Table A.1 Long Call Example

Long Call Example	
Strategy: Buy a call option.	
Entry Date: 9/24/02	***Underlying Stock:*** XYZ
Expiration Month: Jan 03	***Stock Price:*** 50
Strike Price: 50	***Call Premium:*** 6.50
Maximum Reward: Unlimited to the upside above the breakeven	***Maximum Risk:*** \$650 Limited to call premium. 6.50 × 100 = \$650. Call premium × 100
Breakeven: 56.50 50 + 6.50 = 56.50 Strike price + call premium	***Exit Strategy:*** Close position if it doubles in value, or after a 50% profit. Close position 30 days to expiration.
Reasons for Taking Trade: Bullish market where a rise above the breakeven is anticipated.	***Technical Analysis:*** Bullish trend line, low volatility prior to a rise in volatility.

Long Call: Buy 1 Jan 03 XYZ 50 Call @ 6.50

Date	**Stock Price**	**Call Premium**	**Long Call Profit or Loss**
9/21	50	6.50	(\$650)
9/28	49	5	(\$150)
10/5	51	7	\$50
10/12	54	8.25	\$175
10/19	58	11.25	\$475

Exit the Position: Sell a Jan 03 XYZ 50 call at a profit.

***Final Profit* = \$475**

Events That Influenced Stock Movement

9/27—XYZ announces earnings warning.
10/5—Sector rises above average.
10/11—XYZ releases earnings higher than warning.
10/18—Massive rally across the board.

Table A.2 Long Call Template

Long Call Template	
Strategy: Buy a call option.	
Entry Date:	***Underlying Stock:***
Expiration Month:	***Stock Price:***
Strike Price:	***Call Premium:***
Maximum Reward: Unlimited above the upside breakeven	***Maximum Risk:*** Call premium × 100
Breakeven: Strike price + call premium	***Exit Strategy:***
Reasons for Taking Trade:	***Technical Analysis:***

Long Call:

Date	Stock Price	Call Premium	Long Call Profit or Loss
Exit the Position: ***Final Profit/Loss =***			
Events That Influenced Stock Movement			

Table A.3 Long Put Example

<table>
<tr><th colspan="2">Long Put Example</th></tr>
<tr><td colspan="2">Strategy: Buy a put option.</td></tr>
<tr><td>Entry Date: 9/24/02</td><td>Underlying Stock: XYZ</td></tr>
<tr><td>Expiration Month: Jan 03</td><td>Stock Price: 60</td></tr>
<tr><td>Strike Price: 60</td><td>Put Premium: 6.50</td></tr>
<tr><td>Maximum Reward: Limited below the breakeven as the stock falls to zero.</td><td>Maximum Risk: $650
Limited to put premium.
6.50 × 100 = $650.
Put premium × 100</td></tr>
<tr><td>Breakeven: 53.50
60 – 6.50 = 53.50
Strike price – put premium</td><td>Exit Strategy: Close position if it doubles in value, or after a 50% profit. Close position 30 days to expiration.</td></tr>
<tr><td>Reasons for Taking Trade: Bearish market where you anticipate a fall in the price of the underlying below the breakeven.</td><td>Technical Analysis: Bearish trend, low volatility prior to a rise in volatility.</td></tr>
<tr><td colspan="2">Long Put: Buy 1 Jan 03 XYZ 60 Put @ 6.50</td></tr>
</table>

Date	Stock Price	Put Premium	Long Put Profit or Loss
9/21	60	6.50	($650)
9/28	61	5	($150)
10/5	58	7.25	$75
10/12	55	9	$250
10/19	50	12.25	$575

Exit the Position: Sell a Jan 03 XYZ 60 call at a profit.

***Final Profit* = $575**

Events That Influenced Stock Movement
9/27—XYZ announces earnings.
10/5—Sector falls below average.
10/11—XYZ releases earnings lower than announcement.
10/18—Massive selling across the board.

Table A.4 Long Put Template

Long Put Template	
Strategy: Buy a put option.	
Entry Date:	***Underlying Stock:***
Expiration Month:	***Stock Price:***
Strike Price:	***Put Premium:***
Maximum Reward: Limited below the breakeven as the stock falls to zero.	***Maximum Risk:*** Put premium × 100
Breakeven: Strike price – put premium	***Exit Strategy:***
Reasons for Taking Trade:	***Technical Analysis:***

Long Put:

Date	Stock Price	Put Premium	Long Put Profit or Loss
Exit the Position: ***Final Profit/Loss =***			
Events That Influenced Stock Movement			

Table A.5 Protective Put Example

Protective Put Example	
Strategy: Buy 100 shares of stock and buy an ATM put option.	
Entry Date: 9/24/02	***Underlying Stock:*** XYZ
Expiration Month: Jan 03	***Stock Price:*** 50
Strike Price: 50	***Put Premium:*** 3.75
Maximum Reward: Unlimited as the stock moves higher.	***Maximum Risk:*** $375 [(50 – 50) + 3.75] × 100 = $375 [(Stock price – strike price) + put premium] × 100
Breakeven: 53.75 50 + 3.75 = 53.75 Stock price + put premium	***Exit Strategy:*** If the stock declines, exercise the put to sell it at the initial stock price, incurring only the loss of the put premium.
Reasons for Taking Trade: XYZ is a volatile stock with serious risk in simply owning shares. Put has low IV and can be purchased cheaply to hedge the long stock position.	***Technical Analysis:*** XYZ appears to be consolidating, which means it is ready for a breakout, hopefully to the upside.

Protective Put: Long 100 Shares of XYZ @ 50 and Long 1 Jan 03 XYZ 50 Put @ 3.75

Date	Stock Price	Number of Shares	Long Stock Net Profit/Loss	Long Put Premium	Long Put Net Profit/Loss	Net Profit/Loss on Trade
9/24	50	100	n/a	3.75	($375)	($375)
10/7	52	100	$200	3.25	($50)	$150
10/14	55	100	$500	2.75	($100)	$400
10/28	48	100	($200)	4.25	$50	($150)
11/4	42	100	($800)	5.75	$200	($600)
11/5	41	100	($900)	6	$225	($675)

Exit the Position: Exercise the put to sell XYZ at $50 a share.

***Final Loss* = $375** (put premium)

Events That Influenced Stock Movement
10/7—XYZ releases positive earnings report—meets expectations.
10/14—Rumors of merger.
10/28—Merger denied, stock falls on the news.
11/4—Accounting irregularities reported in press.

Table A.6 Protective Put Template

Protective Put Template	
Strategy: Buy 100 shares of stock and buy an ATM put option.	
Entry Date:	***Underlying Stock:***
Expiration Month:	***Stock Price:***
Strike Price:	***Put Premium:***
Maximum Reward: Unlimited as the stock moves higher.	***Maximum Risk:*** [(Stock price – strike price) + put premium] × 100
Breakeven: Stock price + put option premium	***Exit Strategy:***
Reasons for Taking Trade:	***Technical Analysis:***

Protective Put:

Date	Stock Price	Number of Shares	Long Stock Net Profit/Loss	Long Put Premium	Long Put Net Profit/Loss	Net Profit/Loss on Trade

Exit the Position:

Final Profit/Loss =

Events That Influenced Stock Movement

Table A.7 Covered Call Example

<table>
<tr><th colspan="7">Covered Call Example</th></tr>
<tr><td colspan="7">Strategy: Sell an OTM call with 30 to 45 days to expiration against 100 long shares of the underlying stock.</td></tr>
<tr><td colspan="3">Entry Date: 9/24/02</td><td colspan="4">Underlying Stock: XYZ</td></tr>
<tr><td colspan="3">Expiration Month: Oct 02</td><td colspan="4">Stock Price: 90.50 or $9,050 for 100 shares</td></tr>
<tr><td colspan="3">Short Strike Price to Sell: 95</td><td colspan="4">Short Call Premium: 6.50</td></tr>
<tr><td colspan="3">Maximum Reward: $1,100
[(95 – 90.50) × 100] + 650 = $1,100
[(Strike price – initial stock price) × 100] + short call credit</td><td colspan="4">Maximum Risk: Limited to the downside below the breakeven as the stock falls to zero</td></tr>
<tr><td colspan="3">Breakeven: 84
90.50 – 6.50 = 84
Initial stock price – call premium</td><td colspan="4">Exit Strategy: 50% of profit potential ($550) or if position loses 50% of premium paid.</td></tr>
<tr><td colspan="3">Reasons for Taking Trade: Slightly bullish to neutral stock. A slow rise with little chance of a reversal.</td><td colspan="4">Technical Analysis: Short-term sideways market strength.</td></tr>
<tr><td colspan="7">Covered Call: Own 100 shares XYZ Stock @ 90.50 & Short 1 Oct XYZ 95 Call @ 6.50</td></tr>
<tr><th>Date</th><th>Stock Price</th><th>Number of Shares</th><th>Long Stock/Net Profit/Loss</th><th>Short Call Premium</th><th>Short Call Net Profit/Loss</th><th>Net Profit or Loss</th></tr>
<tr><td>9/21</td><td>90.55</td><td>100</td><td>0</td><td>6.50</td><td>$650</td><td>$650</td></tr>
<tr><td>9/28</td><td>87.80</td><td>100</td><td>($275)</td><td>2.50</td><td>$400</td><td>$125</td></tr>
<tr><td>10/5</td><td>85.45</td><td>100</td><td>($510)</td><td>1.00</td><td>$550</td><td>$40</td></tr>
<tr><td>10/12</td><td>90.75</td><td>100</td><td>$20</td><td>3.80</td><td>$270</td><td>$290</td></tr>
<tr><td>10/19</td><td>94.85</td><td>100</td><td>$430</td><td>.25</td><td>$625</td><td>$1,055</td></tr>
<tr><td colspan="7">Exit the Position: Let the short call expire worthless and hold onto the XYZ shares to sell another covered call against.
Final Profit = $650 (call premium)</td></tr>
<tr><td colspan="7">Events That Influenced Stock Movement
9/24—Stock bounces off resistance.
9/27—XYZ announces earnings warning.
10/5—Sector falls below average.
10/11—XYZ releases earnings higher than warning.
10/18—Massive rally across the board.</td></tr>
</table>

Table A.8 Covered Call Template

Covered Call Template	
Strategy: Sell an OTM call with 30 to 45 days to expiration against 100 long shares of the underlying stock.	
Entry Date:	***Underlying Stock:***
Expiration Month:	***Stock Price:***
Short Strike Price to Sell:	***Short Call Premium:***
Maximum Reward: [(Strike price – initial stock price) × 100] + short call credit	***Maximum Risk:*** Limited to the downside below the breakeven as the stock falls to zero
Breakeven: Initial stock price – call premium	***Exit Strategy:***
Reasons for Taking Trade:	***Technical Analysis:***
Covered Call:	

Date	Stock Price	Number of Shares	Long Stock Net Profit/Loss	Short Call Premium	Short Call Net Profit/Loss	Net Profit or Loss

Exit the Position:

Final Profit/Loss =

Events That Influenced Stock Movement

Table A.9 Bull Call Spread Example

Bull Call Spread Example	
Strategy: Buy a lower strike call and sell a higher strike call with the same expiration.	
Entry Date: 9/21/02	***Underlying Stock:*** XYZ
Expiration Month: Jan 03	***Stock Price:*** 90.50
Lower Strike Price to Buy: 85	***Long Call Premium:*** 12 80 or $1,280
Higher Strike Price to Sell: 95	***Short Call Premium:*** 7.80 or $780
Maximum Risk: $500 [(12.80 – 7.80) × 100] = $500 (Long – short premium) × 100 = net debit	***Maximum Reward:*** $500 [(95 – 85) × 100] – 500 = $500 (Difference in strikes × 100) – net debit
Breakeven: 90 85 + 5 = 90 Lower strike price + net debit	***Exit Strategy:*** Close out the position if you make 50% of profit potential. If you have more than one contract, close out half of the position if it doubles in value. Close out the remainder at 80% of its maximum spread. Either way, close out the entire trade at 30 days to expiration.
Reasons for Taking Trade: Strong fundamentals. Low implied volatility on options. Long-term growth appears secure. Low volatility stock.	***Technical Analysis:*** Current bearish trend likely to reverse—capitulation in the works. Bollinger bands narrowing.
Bull Call Spread: Long 1 Jan XYZ 85 Call @ 12.80 and Short 1 Jan XYZ 95 Call @ 7.80	

Date	Stock Price	Number of Spreads	Long Call Premium	Long Call Net Profit/Loss	Short Call Premium	Short Call Net Profit/Loss	Net Profit or Loss
9/21	90.50	1	12.80	0	7.80	0	($500)
9/24	92.00	1	14.00	$120	8.50	($70)	$50
10/1	95.00	1	15.10	$230	9.10	($130)	$100
10/8	98.50	1	17.20	$440	10	($220)	$220
10/16	101	1	21.50	$870	11.70	($390)	$480

Exit the Position: Sell long 85 call at a profit and buy back 95 call for a loss.
Final Profit = $480

Events That Influenced Stock Movement
9/24—Tech stocks rally.
10/1—XYZ beats the Street's whisper number for earnings.
10/8—Nasdaq continues to rally. PPI more positive than expected.
10/15—Dell inspires tech rally.

Table A.10 Bull Call Spread Template

Bull Call Spread Template	
Strategy: Buy a lower strike call and sell a higher strike call with the same expiration.	
Entry Date:	***Underlying Stock:***
Expiration Month:	***Stock Price:***
Lower Strike Price to Buy:	***Long Call Premium:***
Higher Strike Price to Sell:	***Short Call Premium:***
Maximum Risk: (Long – short premium) × 100 = net debit	***Maximum Reward:*** (Difference in strikes × 100) – net debit
Breakeven: Lower strike price + net debit	***Exit Strategy:***
Reasons for Taking Trade:	***Technical Analysis:***

Bull Call Spread:

Date	Stock Price	Number of Spreads	Long Call Premium	Long Call Net Profit/Loss	Short Call Premium	Short Call Net Profit/Loss	Net Profit or Loss

Exit the Position:

Final Profit/Loss =

Events That Influenced Stock Movement

Table A.11 Bear Put Spread Example

Bear Put Spread Example	
Strategy: Buy a higher strike put and sell a lower strike put with the same expiration.	
Entry Date: 9/21/02	***Underlying Stock:*** XYZ
Expiration Month: Dec 02	***Stock Price:*** 58.04
Higher Strike Price to Buy: 60	***Long Put Premium:*** 4.50
Lower Strike Price to Sell: 50	***Short Put Premium:*** 1.20
Maximum Risk: $330 (4.50 – 1.20) × 100 = $330 (Long – short premium) × 100 = net debit	***Maximum Reward:*** $670 [(60 – 50) x 100] – 330 = $670 (Difference in strikes × 100) – net debit
Breakeven: 56.70 (60 – 3.30 = 56.70) Higher strike price – net debit	***Exit Strategy:*** Close out the position if you make 50% of profit potential. If you have more than one contract, close out half of the position if it doubles in value. Close out the remainder at 80% of its maximum spread. Either way, close out the entire trade at 30 days to expiration.
Reasons for Taking Trade: A bearish market where a modest decrease in the price of the underlying stock is anticipated. Low volatility stock.	***Technical Analysis:*** Double top forming at resistance, stock looks poised to fall back to support.
Bear Put Spread: Long 1 Dec XYZ 60 Put @ 4.50 and Short 1 Dec XYZ 50 Put @ 1.20	

Date	Stock Price	Number of Spreads	Long Put Premium	Long Put Net Profit/Loss	Short Put Premium	Short Put Net Profit/Loss	Net Profit or Loss
9/21	58.04	1	4.50	0	1.20	0	($330)
9/28	56.50	1	7.20	$270	2.20	($100)	$170
10/5	60.00	1	3.50	($100)	.75	$45	($55)
10/12	57.35	1	6.00	$250	2.10	($90)	$160
10/19	55.40	1	9.10	$460	3.35	($215)	$245
10/26	52.75	1	12.80	$830	4.40	($320)	$510

Exit the Position: Sell the 60 put at a profit and buy back the 50 put at a loss.
Final Profit = $510

Events That Influenced Stock Movement
9/21—Congress approves additional tax cut.
9/27—15,000 job cuts by AOL.
10/5—Unemployment report shows lower job loss than expected.
10/11—Fed rate cut, but market doesn't react.
10/20—Earnings warnings drive Dow and Nasdaq lower.
10/25—CPI shows consumer sentiment dropping fast.

Table A.12 Bear Put Spread Template

Bear Put Spread Template	
Strategy: Buy a higher strike put and sell a lower strike put with the same expiration.	
Entry Date:	***Underlying Stock:***
Expiration Month:	***Stock Price:***
Higher Strike Price to Buy:	***Long Put Premium:***
Lower Strike Price to Sell:	***Short Put Premium:***
Maximum Risk: (Long – short premium) × 100 = net debit	***Maximum Reward:*** (Difference in strikes × 100) – net debit
Breakeven: Higher strike price – net debit	***Exit Strategy:***
Reasons for Taking Trade:	***Technical Analysis:***

Bear Put Spread:

Date	Stock Price	Number of Spreads	Long Put Premium	Long Put Net Profit/Loss	Short Put Premium	Short Put Net Profit/Loss	Net Profit or Loss

Exit the Position:

Final Profit/Loss =

Events That Influenced Stock Movement

Table A.13 Bull Put Spread Example

Bull Put Spread Example	
Strategy: Buy a lower strike put and sell a higher strike put with the same expiration.	
Entry Date: 9/21/02	***Underlying Stock:*** XYZ
Expiration Month: Oct 02	***Stock Price:*** 50.27
Lower Strike to Buy: 50	***Long Put Premium:*** 5.50
Higher Strike to Sell: 60	***Short Put Premium:*** 11.70
Maximum Risk: $380 [(60 – 50) × 100] – 620 = $380 (Difference in strikes x 100) – net credit	***Maximum Reward:*** $620 [(11.70 – 5.50) × 100] = $620 (Short – long premium) × 100 = net credit
Breakeven: 53.80 (60 – 6.20 = 53.80) Higher strike price – net credit	***Exit Strategy:*** Let the short option expire worthless and keep the net credit.
Reasons for Taking Trade: Stock holding steady; earnings close to announcements. High volatility stock.	***Technical Analysis:*** Positive trend that is approaching the third Elliott Wave.

Bull Put Spread: Long 1 Oct XYZ 50 Put @ 5.50 and Short 1 Oct XYZ 60 Put @ 11.70

Date	Stock Price	Number of Spreads	Long Put Premium	Long Put Net Profit/Loss	Short Put Premium	Short Put Net Profit/Loss	Net Profit or Loss
9/21	50.27	1	5.50	($550)	11.70	$1,170	n/a
9/28	51.00	1	4.75	($75)	11.25	$45	($30)
10/5	47.90	1	6.50	$100	14.50	($280)	($180)
10/12	54.00	1	3.75	($175)	7.50	$420	$245
10/19	56.75	1	.50	($500)	3.50	$820	$320

Exit the Position: Let both options expire worthless and keep the net credit.

***Final Profit* = $620** (net credit)

Events That Influenced Stock Movement
9/20—Earnings warning less than expected.
9/27—Fed cuts rates, inspires rally.
10/4—Sector falls on poor earnings from similar companies.
10/11—Company announces new CEO.

Table A.14 Bull Put Spread Template

<table>
<tr><th colspan="2">Bull Put Spread Template</th></tr>
<tr><td colspan="2">Strategy: Buy a lower strike put and sell a higher strike put with the same expiration.</td></tr>
<tr><td>Entry Date:</td><td>Underlying Stock:</td></tr>
<tr><td>Expiration Month:</td><td>Stock Price:</td></tr>
<tr><td>Lower Strike Price to Buy:</td><td>Long Put Premium:</td></tr>
<tr><td>Higher Strike Price to Sell:</td><td>Short Put Premium:</td></tr>
<tr><td>Maximum Risk:

(Difference in strikes × 100) – net credit</td><td>Maximum Reward:

(Short – long premium) × 100 = net credit</td></tr>
<tr><td>Breakeven:

Higher strike price – net credit</td><td>Exit Strategy:</td></tr>
<tr><td>Reasons for Taking Trade:</td><td>Technical Analysis:</td></tr>
<tr><td colspan="2">Bull Put Spread:</td></tr>
</table>

Date	Stock Price	Number of Spreads	Long Put Premium	Long Put Net Profit/Loss	Short Put Premium	Short Put Net Profit/Loss	Net Profit or Loss

Exit the Position:

Final Profit/Loss =

Events That Influenced Stock Movement

Table A.15 Bear Call Spread Example

Bear Call Spread Example	
Strategy: Buy a higher strike call and sell a lower strike call with the same expiration.	
Entry Date: 9/21/02	***Underlying Stock:*** XYZ
Expiration Month: Oct 02	***Stock Price:*** 33.16
Higher Strike to Buy: 35	***Long Call Premium:*** 1.90
Lower Strike to Sell: 30	***Short Call Premium:*** 4.90
Maximum Risk: $200 [(35 – 30) × 100] – 300 = $200 (Difference in strikes x 100) – net credit	***Maximum Reward:*** $300 [(4.90 – 1.90) x 100] = $300 (Short – long premium) x 100 = net credit
Breakeven: 33 (30 + 3 = 33) Lower strike price + net credit	***Exit Strategy:*** Allow options to expire worthless and keep the net credit of $300. If stock starts to climb past the higher strike, exit the position.
Reasons for Taking Trade: Earnings warning driving stock down. Sector is also in a slump. High volatility stock.	***Technical Analysis:*** Recent positive trend is reversing. Oscillator shows stock is overbought.

Bear Call Spread: Long 1 Oct XYZ 35 Call @ 1.90 and Short 1 Oct XYZ 30 Call @ 4.90

Date	Stock Price	Number of Spreads	Long Call Premium	Long Call Net Profit/Loss	Short Call Premium	Short Call Net Profit/Loss	Net Profit or Loss
9/21	33.16	1	1.90	($190)	4.90	$490	n/a
9/28	35.80	1	3.10	$120	6.75	($185)	($65)
10/5	32.80	1	1.80	($10)	5.20	($30)	($40)
10/12	30.20	1	1.00	($90)	2.75	$215	$125
10/19	29.80	1	.25	($165)	.25	$465	$300

Exit the Position: Let both options expire worthless and keep the net credit.

***Final Profit* = $300** (net credit)

Events That Influenced Stock Movement
9/27—Fed cuts interest rates by a half point.
10/3—XYZ announces 5,000 employee layoffs.
10/11—CEO of XYZ resigns.

Table A.16 Bear Call Spread Template

Bear Call Spread Template	
Strategy: Buy a higher strike call and sell a lower strike call with the same expiration.	
Entry Date:	***Underlying Stock:***
Expiration Month:	***Stock Price:***
Higher Strike to Buy:	***Long Call Premium:***
Lower Strike to Sell:	***Short Call Premium:***
Maximum Risk: (Difference in strikes × 100) – net credit	***Maximum Reward:*** (Short – long premium) × 100 = net credit
Breakeven: Lower strike price + net credit	***Exit Strategy:***
Reasons for Taking Trade:	***Technical Analysis:***

Bear Call Spread:

Date	Stock Price	Number of Spreads	Long Call Premium	Long Call Net Profit/Loss	Short Call Premium	Short Call Net Profit/Loss	Net Profit or Loss

Exit the Position:

Final Profit/Loss =

Events That Influenced Stock Movement

Table A.17 Call Ratio Backspread Example

<table>
<tr><th colspan="2">Call Ratio Backspread Example</th></tr>
<tr><td colspan="2">Strategy: Sell lower strike calls and buy a greater number of higher strike calls with the same expiration with a ratio less than 2/3.</td></tr>
<tr><td>Entry Date: 10/01/02</td><td>Underlying Stock: XYZ</td></tr>
<tr><td>Expiration Month: Jan 03</td><td>Stock Price: 73.45</td></tr>
<tr><td>Higher Strike to Buy: 70</td><td># × Long Call Premium: 3 × 7.40</td></tr>
<tr><td>Lower Strike to Sell: 65</td><td># × Short Call Premium: 2 × 11.10</td></tr>
<tr><td>Maximum Risk: $1,000
[(2 × 5) × 100] – 0 = $1,000
[(# short calls × difference in strikes) × 100] – net credit (or + net debit)</td><td>Maximum Reward: $0
Unlimited to the upside beyond the breakeven. Limited to the net credit to the downside.
Net credit/debit = [(2 × 11.10) – (3 × 7.40) × 100] = 0</td></tr>
<tr><td>Downside Breakeven: 65
65 + 0 = 65
Lower strike price + net credit (or – net debit)</td><td>Upside Breakeven: 80
70 + [(70 – 65) × 2] / (3 – 2) – 0 = 80
Higher strike + [(difference in strikes × # of short calls)/(# of long calls – # of short calls)] – net credit (or + net debit)</td></tr>
<tr><td>Reasons for Taking Trade: Anticipate a sharply rising market and an increase in volatility.</td><td>Exit Strategy: If a 50% profit is reached, offset the short calls and an equal number of long calls. Hold onto the other long option for additional profit. Or simply close out the whole position if you make twice the maximum risk.
If you lose 50%, exit the position.</td></tr>
<tr><td colspan="2">Call Ratio Backspread: Short 2 Jan 03 XYZ 65 Calls @ 11.10 and Long 3 Jan 03 XYZ 70 Calls @ 7.40</td></tr>
</table>

Date	Stock Price	Ratio (Short to Long)	Long Call Premium	Long Call Value	Short Call Premium	Short Call Value	Net Profit or Loss
10/1	73.45	2 to 3	7.40	$2,220	11.10	$2,220	0
10/8	75.00	2 to 3	8.00	$2,400	13.20	$2,640	($240)
10/15	80.00	2 to 3	11.00	$3,300	16.50	$3,300	$0
10/22	86.00	2 to 3	19.50	$5,850	24.10	$4,820	$1,030
10/29	94.50	2 to 3	32.20	$9,660	35.10	$7,020	$2,640

Exit the Position: Buy 2 Jan XYZ 65 calls and sell 3 Jan XYZ 70 calls.
Final Profit = $2,640

Events That Influenced Stock Movement
10/2—Fed lowers interest rates 50 basis points.
10/10—Surge in health care sector boosts prices.
10/23—Earnings report released; earnings up.

Table A.18 Call Ratio Backspread Template

<table>
<tr><th colspan="2">Call Ratio Backspread Template</th></tr>
<tr><td colspan="2">Strategy: Sell lower strike calls and buy a greater number of higher strike calls with the same expiration with a ratio less than 2/3.</td></tr>
<tr><td>Entry Date:</td><td>Underlying Stock:</td></tr>
<tr><td>Expiration Month:</td><td>Stock Price:</td></tr>
<tr><td>Higher Strike to Buy:</td><td># × Long Call Premium:</td></tr>
<tr><td>Lower Strike to Sell:</td><td># × Short Call Premium:</td></tr>
<tr><td>Maximum Risk:

[(# short calls × difference in strikes) × 100] – net credit (or + net debit)</td><td>Maximum Reward:
Unlimited to the upside beyond the breakeven. Limited to the net credit to the downside.
Net debit/credit =</td></tr>
<tr><td>Downside Breakeven:

Short strike price + net credit (or – net debit)</td><td>Upside Breakeven:

Higher strike +[(difference in strikes × # of short calls) divided by (# of long calls – # of short calls)] – net credit (or + net debit)</td></tr>
<tr><td>Reasons for Taking Trade:</td><td>Exit Strategy:</td></tr>
<tr><td colspan="2">Call Ratio Backspread:</td></tr>
</table>

Date	Stock Price	Ratio (Short to Long)	Long Call Premium	Long Call Value	Short Call Premium	Short Call Value	Net Profit or Loss

Exit the Position:

Final Profit/Loss =

Events That Influenced Stock Movement

Table A.19 Put Ratio Backspread Example

<table>
<tr><th colspan="2">Put Ratio Backspread Example</th></tr>
<tr><td colspan="2">Strategy: Sell higher strike puts and buy a greater number of lower strike puts with the same expiration with a ratio less than ²/₃.</td></tr>
<tr><td>Entry Date: 10/1/02</td><td>Underlying Stock: XYZ</td></tr>
<tr><td>Expiration Month: Jan 03</td><td>Stock Price: 30.61</td></tr>
<tr><td>Higher Strike to Sell: 35</td><td># × Short Put Premium: 1 × 6.40 = 6.40</td></tr>
<tr><td>Lower Strike to Buy: 30</td><td># × Long Put Premium: 2 × 3.20 = 6.40</td></tr>
<tr><td>Maximum Risk: $1,000
[(2 × 5) × 100] – 0 = $1,000
[(# short puts × difference in strikes) × 100] – net credit (or + net debit)</td><td>Maximum Reward:
Limited to the downside below the breakeven as the stock falls to zero. Limited to the net credit to the upside.
Net credit/debit = [(1 × 6.40) – (2 × 3.20) × 100] = 0</td></tr>
<tr><td>Upside Breakeven: 35
35 – 0 = 35
Higher strike price – net credit (or + net debit)</td><td>Downside Breakeven: 25
30 – [(5 × 1)/(2 – 1)] + 0 = 25
Lower strike – [(difference in strikes × # of short puts)/(# of long puts – # of short puts)] + net credit (or – net debit)</td></tr>
<tr><td>Reasons for Taking Trade: Anticipate a sharply rising market and an increase in volatility.</td><td>Exit Strategy: If a 50% profit is reached, close out the short put and an equal number of long puts. Hold onto the other long put option for additional profit. Or simply close out the whole position if you make twice the maximum risk. If you lose 50%, exit the position.</td></tr>
<tr><td colspan="2">Put Ratio Backspread: Short 1 Jan XYZ 35 Put @ 6.40 and Long 2 Jan XYZ 30 Puts @ 3.20</td></tr>
</table>

Date	Stock Price	Ratio (Short to Long)	Long Put Premium	Long Put Value	Short Put Premium	Short Put Value	Net Profit or Loss
10/1	30.61	1 to 2	3.20	$640	6.40	$640	0
10/8	35.10	1 to 2	1.50	$300	4.70	$470	($170)
10/15	30.20	1 to 2	3.30	$660	7.30	$730	($70)
10/22	27.00	1 to 2	4.50	$900	9.50	$950	($50)
10/29	23.50	1 to 2	8.10	$1,620	11. 20	$1,120	$500
11/5	20.80	1 to 2	14.60	$2,920	17.60	$1,760	$1,160

Exit the Position: Sell 2 Jan XYZ 30 puts and buy 1 Jan XYZ 35 put.
***Final Profit* = $1,160**

Events That Influenced Stock Movement
10/9—OPEC meeting cuts production of oil to boost prices.
10/18—Consumer confidence and GNP drop significantly.
10/24—Accounting irregularities cited in XYZ's quarterly report.

Table A.20 Put Ratio Backspread Template

<table>
<tr><th colspan="8">Put Ratio Backspread Template</th></tr>
<tr><td colspan="8">Strategy: Sell higher strike puts and buy a greater number of lower strike puts with the same expiration with a ratio less than $^{2}/_{3}$.</td></tr>
<tr><td colspan="4">Entry Date:</td><td colspan="4">Underlying Stock:</td></tr>
<tr><td colspan="4">Expiration Month:</td><td colspan="4">Stock Price:</td></tr>
<tr><td colspan="4">Higher Strike to Sell:</td><td colspan="4"># × Short Call Premium:</td></tr>
<tr><td colspan="4">Lower Strike to Buy:</td><td colspan="4"># × Long Call Premium:</td></tr>
<tr><td colspan="4">Maximum Risk:

[(# short puts × difference in strikes) × 100] – net credit (or + net debit)</td><td colspan="4">Maximum Reward:
Limited to the downside below the breakeven as the stock falls to zero.
Limited to the net credit to the upside.
Net debit/credit:</td></tr>
<tr><td colspan="4">Upside Breakeven:

Higher strike price – net credit (or + net debit)</td><td colspan="4">Downside Breakeven:

Lower strike – [(difference in strikes × # of short puts) divided by (# of long puts – # of short puts)] + net credit (or – net debit)</td></tr>
<tr><td colspan="4">Reasons for Taking Trade:</td><td colspan="4">Exit Strategy:</td></tr>
<tr><td colspan="8">Put Ratio Backspread:</td></tr>
<tr><th>Date</th><th>Stock Price</th><th>Ratio (Short to Long)</th><th>Long Put Premium</th><th>Long Put Value</th><th>Short Put Premium</th><th>Short Put Value</th><th>Net Profit or Loss</th></tr>
<tr><td></td><td></td><td></td><td></td><td></td><td></td><td></td><td></td></tr>
<tr><td></td><td></td><td></td><td></td><td></td><td></td><td></td><td></td></tr>
<tr><td></td><td></td><td></td><td></td><td></td><td></td><td></td><td></td></tr>
<tr><td></td><td></td><td></td><td></td><td></td><td></td><td></td><td></td></tr>
<tr><td></td><td></td><td></td><td></td><td></td><td></td><td></td><td></td></tr>
<tr><td></td><td></td><td></td><td></td><td></td><td></td><td></td><td></td></tr>
<tr><td colspan="8">Exit the Position:

Final Profit/Loss =</td></tr>
<tr><td colspan="8">Events That Influenced Stock Movement</td></tr>
</table>

Table A.21 Long Straddle Example

Long Straddle Example

Strategy: Buy an equal number of puts and calls with the same at-the-money strike price and expiration month.

Entry Date: 9/21/02	***Underlying Stock:*** XYZ
Expiration Month and Strike: Jan 03 75	***Stock Price:*** 73.50
ATM Call Premium to Buy: 3.60	***ATM Put Premium to Buy:*** 4.70
Maximum Reward: Unlimited beyond upside breakeven and limited as the stock falls below the downside breakeven all the way to zero.	***Maximum Risk:*** \$830 (3.60 + 4.70) × 100 = \$830 (Call + put premium) × 100 = net debit
Upside Breakeven: 83.30 75 + 8.30 = 83.30 Strike price + net debit	***Downside Breakeven:*** 66.70 75 – 8.30 = 66.70 Strike price – net debit
Reasons for Taking Trade: Low volatility in options; volume slowly increasing. Earnings report due out in two weeks. The price is consolidating, which means a price breakout seems likely.	***Exit Strategy:*** Exit with a 50% profit (or loss). Close out the entire trade at 30 days to expiration.

Long Straddle: Long 1 Jan 03 XYZ 75 Call @ 3.60 and Long 1 Jan 03 XYZ 75 Put @ 4.70

Date	Stock Price	Number of Straddles	Long Call Premium	Long Call Net Profit/Loss	Long Put Premium	Short Put Net Profit/Loss	Net Profit or Loss
9/21	73.50	1	3.60	(\$360)	7.70	(\$470)	(\$830)
9/28	71.85	1	2.00	(\$160)	5.50	\$80	(\$80)
10/5	70.25	1	1.75	(\$185)	6.15	\$145	(\$40)
10/12	74.50	1	4.80	\$120	3.20	(\$150)	(\$30)
10/19	80.45	1	7.60	\$400	.50	(\$420)	(\$20)
10/26	86.50	1	14.50	\$1,090	.25	(\$445)	\$645

Exit the Position: Sell the long call for a profit and hold onto the long put just in case XYZ reverses, thereby increasing the value on the long put.
Final Profit = \$645

Events That Influenced Stock Movement
9/27—Prices consolidating; management shake-up.
10/4—Earnings warning released.
10/11—New CEO announced.
10/19—Contract to supply parts to a Chinese manufacturer.
10/25—Several analysts upgrade XYZ from "hold" to "buy."

Table A.22 Long Straddle Template

<table>
<tr><th colspan="8">Long Straddle Template</th></tr>
<tr><td colspan="8">Strategy: Buy an equal number of puts and calls with the same at-the-money strike price and expiration month.</td></tr>
<tr><td colspan="4">Entry Date:</td><td colspan="4">Underlying Stock:</td></tr>
<tr><td colspan="4">Expiration Month and Strike:</td><td colspan="4">Stock Price:</td></tr>
<tr><td colspan="4">ATM Call Premium to Buy:</td><td colspan="4">ATM Put Premium to Buy:</td></tr>
<tr><td colspan="4">Maximum Reward:
Unlimited beyond upside breakeven and limited as the stock falls below the downside breakeven all the way to zero.</td><td colspan="4">Maximum Risk:
(Call + put premium) × 100 = net debit</td></tr>
<tr><td colspan="4">Upside Breakeven:
Strike price + net debit</td><td colspan="4">Downside Breakeven:
Strike price – net debit</td></tr>
<tr><td colspan="4">Reasons for Taking Trade:</td><td colspan="4">Exit Strategy:</td></tr>
<tr><td colspan="8">Long Straddle:</td></tr>
<tr><th>Date</th><th>Stock Price</th><th>Number of Straddles</th><th>Long Call Premium</th><th>Long Call Net Profit/Loss</th><th>Long Put Premium</th><th>Short Put Net Profit/Loss</th><th>Net Profit or Loss</th></tr>
<tr><td></td><td></td><td></td><td></td><td></td><td></td><td></td><td></td></tr>
<tr><td></td><td></td><td></td><td></td><td></td><td></td><td></td><td></td></tr>
<tr><td></td><td></td><td></td><td></td><td></td><td></td><td></td><td></td></tr>
<tr><td></td><td></td><td></td><td></td><td></td><td></td><td></td><td></td></tr>
<tr><td></td><td></td><td></td><td></td><td></td><td></td><td></td><td></td></tr>
<tr><td></td><td></td><td></td><td></td><td></td><td></td><td></td><td></td></tr>
<tr><td colspan="8">Exit the Position:
Final Profit/Loss =</td></tr>
<tr><td colspan="8">Events That Influenced Stock Movement</td></tr>
</table>

Table A.23 Long Butterfly Spread Example

Long Butterfly Spread Example

Strategy: Use all calls or all puts. Buy a higher strike at resistance, sell two lower strikes at equilibrium, and buy an even lower strike at support.

Entry Date: 9/21/02	***Underlying Stock:*** XYZ
Expiration Month: Dec 02	***Stock Price:*** 49.90
Highest Strike Option: 55 Call	***Wing—Premium to Buy:*** .90
Middle Strike Option: 50 Call	***Body—Two Premiums to Sell:*** 2.80
Lowest Strike Option: 45 Call	***Wing—Premium to Buy:*** 5.80
Maximum Reward: \$390 [(55 – 50) × 100] – 110 = \$390 [(Higher strike – short strike) × 100] – net debit	***Maximum Risk:*** \$110 [(5.80 + .90) – (2 × 2.80)] × 100 = \$110 (Long – short premiums) × 100 = net debit
Upside Breakeven: 53.90 55 – 1.10 = 53.90 Highest strike price – net debit	***Downside Breakeven:*** 46.10 45 + 1.10 = 46.10 Lowest strike price + net debit
Reasons for Taking Trade: XYZ has been range trading for six months and is continuing to experience high volatility—just hitting resistance and retracing again.	***Exit Strategy:*** Exit when you have a 50% profit. Close out the entire trade at 30 days to expiration.

Long Butterfly Spread: Long 1 Dec XYZ 90 Call @ .90, Short 2 Dec XYZ 50 Calls @ 2.80, and Long 1 Dec XYZ 45 Call @ 5.80

Date	Stock Price	Higher Long Premium	Net Profit/ Loss	Middle Short Premium	Net Profit/ Loss	Lower Long Premium	Net Profit/ Loss	Net Profit/ Loss on Trade
9/21	49.90	.90	(\$580)	2.80	\$560	5.80	(\$580)	(\$110)
10/5	52.75	2.25	\$135	4.50	(\$340)	8.90	\$310	\$105
10/19	54.25	3.10	\$220	7.75	(\$990)	12.25	\$645	(\$125)
10/31	52.85	2.20	\$130	4.25	(\$290)	8.50	\$265	\$110
11/15	48.75	.80	(\$10)	2.50	\$60	5.70	(\$10)	\$40
11/28	50.50	1.25	\$35	2.25	\$55	6.90	\$110	\$200

Exit the Position: Sell the long calls and buy back the short calls for a small overall profit.
Final Profit = \$200

Events That Influenced Stock Movement

9/28—Fed cuts interest rates by 50 basis points.
10/18—Large contract with Mexico in negotiations.
10/30—Contract falls through; stock starts to slide back down again.
11/14—Volume spike increases implied volatility of options.
11/27—Warnings announcement confirms earnings estimate.

Table A.24 Long Butterfly Spread Template

<table>
<tr><th colspan="9">Long Butterfly Spread Template</th></tr>
<tr><td colspan="9">Strategy: Use all calls or all puts. Buy a higher strike at resistance, sell two lower strikes at equilibrium, and buy an even lower strike at support.</td></tr>
<tr><td colspan="4">Entry Date:</td><td colspan="5">Underlying Stock:</td></tr>
<tr><td colspan="4">Expiration Month:</td><td colspan="5">Stock Price:</td></tr>
<tr><td colspan="4">Highest Strike Option:</td><td colspan="5">Wing—Premium to Buy:</td></tr>
<tr><td colspan="4">Middle Strike Option:</td><td colspan="5">Body—Two Premiums to Sell:</td></tr>
<tr><td colspan="4">Lowest Strike Option:</td><td colspan="5">Wing—Premium to Buy:</td></tr>
<tr><td colspan="4">Maximum Reward:

[(Higher strike – short strike) × 100] – net debit</td><td colspan="5">Maximum Risk:

(Long – short premiums) × 100 = net debit</td></tr>
<tr><td colspan="4">Upside Breakeven:

Highest strike price – net debit</td><td colspan="5">Downside Breakeven:

Lowest strike price + net debit</td></tr>
<tr><td colspan="4">Reasons for Taking Trade:</td><td colspan="5">Exit Strategy:</td></tr>
<tr><td colspan="9">Long Butterfly Spread:</td></tr>
<tr><th>Date</th><th>Stock Price</th><th>Higher Long Premium</th><th>Net Profit/ Loss</th><th>Middle Short Premium</th><th>Net Profit/ Loss</th><th>Lower Long Premium</th><th>Net Profit/ Loss</th><th>Net Profit/ Loss on Trade</th></tr>
<tr><td></td><td></td><td></td><td></td><td></td><td></td><td></td><td></td><td></td></tr>
<tr><td></td><td></td><td></td><td></td><td></td><td></td><td></td><td></td><td></td></tr>
<tr><td></td><td></td><td></td><td></td><td></td><td></td><td></td><td></td><td></td></tr>
<tr><td></td><td></td><td></td><td></td><td></td><td></td><td></td><td></td><td></td></tr>
<tr><td></td><td></td><td></td><td></td><td></td><td></td><td></td><td></td><td></td></tr>
<tr><td></td><td></td><td></td><td></td><td></td><td></td><td></td><td></td><td></td></tr>
<tr><td colspan="9">Exit the Position:

Final Profit/Loss =</td></tr>
<tr><td colspan="9">Events That Influenced Stock Movement</td></tr>
</table>

Table A.25 Long Iron Butterfly Spread Example

Long Iron Butterfly Spread Example

Strategy: Buy a higher strike call at resistance, sell an ATM strike call, sell a lower strike put, and buy an even lower strike put at support.

Entry Date: 9/21/02	***Underlying Stock:*** XYZ
Expiration Month: Dec 02	***Stock Price:*** 46.90
Highest Strike Call: 55	***Wing—Premium to Buy:*** 1.45
Middle Strike Call: 50	***Body—Premium to Sell:*** 3.50
Middle Strike Put: 45	***Body—Premium to Sell:*** 3.95
Lowest Strike Put: 40	***Wing—Premium to Buy:*** 1.55
Maximum Reward: $445 [(3.50 + 3.95) – (1.45 + 1.55)] × 100 = $445 (Short – long premiums) × 100 = net credit	***Maximum Risk:*** $55 [(55 – 50) × 100] – 445 = $55 (Difference in strikes × 100) – net credit
Upside Breakeven: 54.45 50 + 4.45 = 54.45 Middle short call strike price + net credit	***Downside Breakeven:*** 40.55 45 – 4.45 = 40.55 Middle short put strike price – net credit
Reasons for Taking Trade: XYZ is a high volatility stock that has been trading in a range between 40 and 55 for more than six months.	***Exit Strategy:*** Exit when you have a 50% profit. Close out the entire trade at 30 days to expiration.

Long Iron Butterfly Spread: Long 1 Dec XYZ 55 Call @ 1.45 and Short 1 Dec XYZ 50 Call @ 3.50; Short 1 Dec XYZ 45 Put @ 3.95 and Long 1 Dec XYZ 40 Put @ 1.55

Date	Stock Price	Long Call Premium	Net Profit/ Loss	Short Call Premium	Net Profit/ Loss	Short Put Premium	Net Profit/ Loss	Long Put Premium	Net Profit/ Loss	Net Profit/ Loss on Trade
9/21	46.90	1.45	($145)	3.50	$350	3.95	$395	1.55	($155)	n/a
9/28	48.75	1.65	$20	3.85	($35)	3.20	$75	1.35	($20)	$40
10/5	52.25	3.00	$155	4.50	($100)	1.75	$120	.85	($70)	$105
10/12	54.75	3.75	$230	6.75	($325)	1.00	$295	.45	($110)	$90
10/19	49.45	2.10	$65	3.25	($25)	2.15	$180	1.55	0	$220

Exit the Position: Sell the long options and buy back the short options.
Final Profit = $220

Events That Influenced Stock Movement
9/27—Fed raises interest rates by 50 basis points.
10/4—Earnings announcement is better than expected.
10/11—Sector strength leads to strong rally.
10/18—Bears return to take profits.

Table A.26 Long Iron Butterfly Spread Template

<table>
<tr><th colspan="11">Long Iron Butterfly Spread Template</th></tr>
<tr><td colspan="11">Strategy: Buy a higher strike call at resistance, sell an ATM strike call, sell a lower strike put, and buy an even lower strike put at support.</td></tr>
<tr><td colspan="5">Entry Date:</td><td colspan="6">Underlying Stock:</td></tr>
<tr><td colspan="5">Expiration Month:</td><td colspan="6">Stock Price:</td></tr>
<tr><td colspan="5">Highest Strike Call:</td><td colspan="6">Wing—Premium to Buy:</td></tr>
<tr><td colspan="5">Middle Strike Call:</td><td colspan="6">Body—Premium to Sell:</td></tr>
<tr><td colspan="5">Middle Strike Put:</td><td colspan="6">Body—Premium to Sell:</td></tr>
<tr><td colspan="5">Lowest Strike Put:</td><td colspan="6">Wing—Premium to Buy:</td></tr>
<tr><td colspan="5">Maximum Reward:

(Short – long premiums) × 100 = net credit</td><td colspan="6">Maximum Risk:

(Difference in strikes × 100) – net credit</td></tr>
<tr><td colspan="5">Upside Breakeven:

Middle short call strike price + net credit</td><td colspan="6">Downside Breakeven:

Middle short put strike price – net credit</td></tr>
<tr><td colspan="5">Reasons for Taking Trade:</td><td colspan="6">Exit Strategy:</td></tr>
<tr><td colspan="11">Long Iron Butterfly Spread:</td></tr>
<tr><th>Date</th><th>Stock Price</th><th>Long Call Premium</th><th>Net Profit/ Loss</th><th>Short Call Premium</th><th>Net Profit/ Loss</th><th>Short Put Premium</th><th>Net Profit/ Loss</th><th>Long Put Premium</th><th>Net Profit/ Loss</th><th>Net Profit/ Loss on Trade</th></tr>
<tr><td></td><td></td><td></td><td></td><td></td><td></td><td></td><td></td><td></td><td></td><td></td></tr>
<tr><td></td><td></td><td></td><td></td><td></td><td></td><td></td><td></td><td></td><td></td><td></td></tr>
<tr><td></td><td></td><td></td><td></td><td></td><td></td><td></td><td></td><td></td><td></td><td></td></tr>
<tr><td></td><td></td><td></td><td></td><td></td><td></td><td></td><td></td><td></td><td></td><td></td></tr>
<tr><td></td><td></td><td></td><td></td><td></td><td></td><td></td><td></td><td></td><td></td><td></td></tr>
<tr><td></td><td></td><td></td><td></td><td></td><td></td><td></td><td></td><td></td><td></td><td></td></tr>
<tr><td colspan="11">Exit the Position:

Final Profit/Loss =</td></tr>
<tr><td colspan="11">Events That Influenced Stock Movement</td></tr>
</table>

Table A.27 Calendar Spread Example

<table>
<tr><th colspan="3">Calendar Spread Example</th></tr>
<tr><td colspan="3">Strategy: Sell a short-term option and buy a long-term option using at-the-money options with as small a net debit as possible. This is a limited risk position that profits as the short front month options (time) decay faster than the long back month options (use all calls or puts).</td></tr>
<tr><td>Entry Date: 9/21/01</td><td colspan="2">Underlying Stock: XYZ</td></tr>
<tr><td>Calls or Puts: Puts</td><td colspan="2">Stock Price: 49.65</td></tr>
<tr><td>Long Option Expiration and Strike: Feb 03 50</td><td>Premium to Buy: 3.65</td><td>IV = 39%</td></tr>
<tr><td>Short Option Expiration and Strike: Oct 50</td><td>Premium to Sell: 2.00</td><td>IV = 78%</td></tr>
<tr><td>Maximum Reward: Varies
Limited (maximum profit potential @ $50 stock price)</td><td colspan="2">Maximum Risk: $165
(3.65 – 2.00) × 100 = $165
(Long – short premium) × 100 = net debit</td></tr>
<tr><td>Upside Breakeven: 53.75</td><td colspan="2">Downside Breakeven: $47.30</td></tr>
<tr><td colspan="3">Accurate assessment of maximum reward and breakevens requires use of option analysis software.</td></tr>
<tr><td>Reasons for Taking Trade: XYZ has been range trading for at least three months and is expected to remain within a range for an extended period of time. Time skew exists.</td><td colspan="2">Exit Strategy: Let the short option expire worthless. Sell another put against the long put in the following month for additional returns.</td></tr>
<tr><td colspan="3">Calendar Spread: Long 1 Oct XYZ 50 Put @ 3.65 and Short 1 Feb 03 XYZ 50 Put @ 2.00</td></tr>
</table>

Date	Stock Price	Long Premium	Long Net Profit/Loss	Short Premium	Short Net Profit/Loss	Net Profit/Loss on Trade
9/21	49.65	3.65	($365)	2.00	$200	($165)
9/28	51.25	3.25	($40)	1.75	$25	$15
10/5	54.00	1.75	($190)	.95	$105	$85
10/12	49.00	4.75	$110	1.50	$50	$160
10/19	50.85	3.50	($15)	.25	$175	$160

Exit the Position: Let the short option expire worthless to keep the full credit; hold the long put and sell a Nov XYZ 50 put to roll the trade forward.
***Interim Profit* = $200** (short put premium)

Events That Influenced Stock Movement
9/27—Fed lowers interest rates by 50 basis points.
10/4—Michigan consumer sentiment index rose, surpassing the previous month.
10/11—Chip stocks sell off, driving market down.
10/18—XYZ releases positive earnings report.

Table A.28 Calendar Spread Template

<table>
<tr><th colspan="7">Calendar Spread Template</th></tr>
<tr><td colspan="7">Strategy: Sell a short-term option and buy a long-term option using at-the-money options with as small a net debit as possible. This is a limited risk position that profits as the short front month options (time) decay faster than the long back month options (use all calls or all puts).</td></tr>
<tr><td colspan="4">Entry Date:</td><td colspan="3">Underlying Stock:</td></tr>
<tr><td colspan="4">Calls or Puts:</td><td colspan="3">Stock Price:</td></tr>
<tr><td colspan="4">Long Option Expiration and Strike:</td><td colspan="2">Premium to Buy:</td><td>IV =</td></tr>
<tr><td colspan="4">Short Option Expiration and Strike:</td><td colspan="2">Premium to Sell:</td><td>IV =</td></tr>
<tr><td colspan="4">Maximum Reward:
Limited (exact maximum potential varies; use software to generate amount)</td><td colspan="3">Maximum Risk:
(Long premium – short premium) × 100 = net debit</td></tr>
<tr><td colspan="4">Upside Breakeven:</td><td colspan="3">Downside Breakeven:</td></tr>
<tr><td colspan="7">Accurate assessment of maximum reward and breakevens requires use of option analysis software.</td></tr>
<tr><td colspan="4">Reasons for Taking Trade:</td><td colspan="3">Exit Strategy:</td></tr>
<tr><td colspan="7">Calendar Spread:</td></tr>
<tr><th>Date</th><th>Stock Price</th><th>Long Premium</th><th>Long Net Profit/Loss</th><th>Short Premium</th><th>Short Net Profit/Loss</th><th>Net Profit/Loss on Trade</th></tr>
<tr><td></td><td></td><td></td><td></td><td></td><td></td><td></td></tr>
<tr><td></td><td></td><td></td><td></td><td></td><td></td><td></td></tr>
<tr><td></td><td></td><td></td><td></td><td></td><td></td><td></td></tr>
<tr><td></td><td></td><td></td><td></td><td></td><td></td><td></td></tr>
<tr><td></td><td></td><td></td><td></td><td></td><td></td><td></td></tr>
<tr><td colspan="7"></td></tr>
<tr><td colspan="7">Exit the Position:

Interim Profit =</td></tr>
<tr><td colspan="7">Events That Influenced Stock Movement</td></tr>
</table>

Table A.29 Diagonal Spread Example

Diagonal Spread Example				
Strategy: Sell a short-term option and buy a long-term option using different strikes with as small a net debit as possible (use all calls or all puts). This spread profits as the short front month options decay faster than the long back month options. For example, a bullish diagonal spread can be created by purchasing a call with a distant expiration and a lower strike price and selling a call with a closer expiration and a higher strike price. A bearish diagonal spread can be created by purchasing a put with a distant expiration and a higher strike price and selling a put with a closer expiration date and a lower strike price. The key is to find options with volatility skews so that you can sell options with high IV and buy options with low IV.				
Entry Date: 9/23/02			***Underlying Stock:*** XYZ ***Stock Price:*** 50	
Option = Calls	***Premium***	***IV***	***Option Strike Price:***	***Expiration Date:***
Long-Term Option	12.75	55%	50	Jan 04
Short-Term Option	2.75	112%	60	Oct 02
Maximum Reward: Varies. Use option analysis software to compute.			***Maximum Risk:*** $1,000 (12.75 – 2.75) × 100 = $1,000 (Long – short premium) × 100 = net debit	
Upside Breakeven: 57.25 Use software to compute.			***Downside Breakeven:*** 47.25 Use software to compute.	
Reasons for Taking Trade: Forward volatility price skew exists. XYZ has been trading in a slightly bullish/sideways channel for more than six months.			***Exit Strategy:*** Let the short call expire to keep the credit and sell another call against the long call in the following month for additional returns.	

Diagonal Spread:

Date	Stock Price	Long Premium	Long Net Profit/Loss	Short Premium	Short Net Profit/Loss	Net Profit/Loss on Trade
9/23	50	12.75	($1,275)	2.75	$275	($1,000)
9/30	52	13.50	$75	2.25	$50	$125
10/7	54	14	$125	2	$75	$200
10/14	52	13	25	.75	$200	$225
10/18	53	13.25	$50	.5	$225	$275

Exit the Position: Let the short put expire to keep the full credit. Sell a Nov 02 XYZ 60 put @ 2.50 against the long put to roll the trade forward.
***Interim Profit* = $275** (short call premium)

Events That Influenced Stock Movement
9/30—Management hires new CEO.
10/7—Fed lowers interest rates.
10/18—Last day short call can be exercised.

Table A.30 Diagonal Spread Template

Diagonal Spread Template

Strategy: Sell a short-term option and buy a long-term option using different strikes with as small a net debit as possible (use all calls or all puts). This spread profits as the short front month options decay faster than the long back month options. For example, a bullish diagonal spread can be created by purchasing a call with a distant expiration and a lower strike price and selling a call with a closer expiration and a higher strike price. A bearish diagonal spread can be created by purchasing a put with a distant expiration and a higher strike price and selling a put with a closer expiration date and a lower strike price. The key is to find options with volatility skews so that you can sell options with high IV and buy options with low IV.

Entry Date:			***Underlying Stock:***	***Stock Price:***
Option =	***Premium***	***IV***	***Option Strike Price:***	***Expiration Date:***
Long-Term Option				
Short-Term Option				

Maximum Reward:	***Maximum Risk:***
Use software to compute.	(Long – short premium) × 100 = net debit
Upside Breakeven: Use software to compute.	***Downside Breakeven:*** Use software to compute.
Reasons for Taking Trade:	***Exit Strategy:***

Diagonal Spread:

Date	Stock Price	Long Premium	Long Net Profit/Loss	Short Premium	Short Net Profit/Loss	Net Profit/Loss on Trade

Exit the Position:

Interim Profit =

Events That Influenced Stock Movement